T0077931

THE PERSISTENT
PASSION
—FOR—
EXCELLENCE

Dr. Herminio L. Gamponia, MD

Order this book online at www.trafford.com
or email orders@trafford.com

Most Trafford titles are also available at major online book retailers.

© Copyright 2020 Dr. Herminio L. Gamponia, MD.
All rights reserved. No part of this publication may be reproduced, stored in a retrieval
system, or transmitted, in any form or by any means, electronic, mechanical, photocopying,
recording, or otherwise, without the written prior permission of the author.

Print information available on the last page.

ISBN: 978-1-6987-0392-3 (sc)
ISBN: 978-1-6987-0394-7 (hc)
ISBN: 978-1-6987-0393-0 (e)

Library of Congress Control Number: 2020920728

Because of the dynamic nature of the Internet, any web addresses or links contained in
this book may have changed since publication and may no longer be valid. The views
expressed in this work are solely those of the author and do not necessarily reflect the
views of the publisher, and the publisher hereby disclaims any responsibility for them.

Any people depicted in stock imagery provided by Getty Images are models, and such images
are being used for illustrative purposes only.
Certain stock imagery © Getty Images.

Trafford rev. 01/27/2021

Trafford
PUBLISHING® www.trafford.com
North America & international
toll-free: 844-688-6899 (USA & Canada)
fax: 812 355 4082

CONTENTS

PART 1

PART 2

ACKNOWLEDGEMENT

I am grateful to my grandson Zachary Wright for doing some correction with my tenses as well as typing part of the manuscript. Jessica G. Write has reviewed the manuscript and emailed it to Trafford Publishing. To my dear wife who is always understanding to use my time in writing.

I am most grateful to Julie Haverty for making many adjustments in the body of the of the manuscript.

INTRODUCTION

- I titled this book "The Persistent Passion for Excellence" because it portrays the many struggles of the author on how he overcame the seemingly impossible coveted goal, to be a medical doctor. I came from a family of seven children, 4 boys and 3 women, thriving only for farming 4 hectares of first- class land which was well irrigated and planted rice twice a year. By the time I was 9 years old, all the elder brothers were already married leaving my 2-year older brother and myself to help our father did the farming. None of the elder brothers went to college. But who could dream that a poor boy can ever go to college since he didn't even have shoes or decent clothes until he was in high school?

- To think of going to college was an impossible dream as even high school required a tuition fee. I had to raise at least 3 piglets and sold them after 6-7 months when they are big enough and the price was enough to pay my tuition. And to go to college with more expensive and required 8 years in college(4 years premed and 4 more years) in the college of medicine. Residency program provides a little incentive but rarely adequate for all the expenses needed. Alberto, my 2-year elder brother and myself have different attitudes. Although we work very hard and willing to shoulder any difficulty just to get things done, the million dollar question remains lingering in my mind. We didn't believe that poverty is a hindrance to college education. And so, my brother went to Manila, Philippines. He found a job washing dishes in Manila hotel during daytime and went to school at night. After 6 years of hard work, he finally graduated from a prominent law school and became a very good lawyer. After several steps of being judge, he was finally appointed to be member of the supreme court. Unfortunately, he was mercilessly murdered while visiting his sugar plantation.

- My strong desire to be a physician didn't prevent me to go to college. But how in the world can I go to college? Where in the world can I get or even borrow any partial amount just to get me enrolled? Please Lord, show me the way.

- I persisted asking God's help and found what I thought to be the solution. My persistent daily prayer brought me to find my God and felt His loving power as if He had assured me to go and pursue medicine as my profession. Yes, I felt deeply strong in my heart as if He was urging me to go ahead and be the best doctor I can ever be. With this in mind, and with very little money, I went to Manila and enrolled to the best school in the country. What was most difficult experience that I felt in my first year college was whether I can take my final examination or not. I was only able to pay half of my tuition fees, and this enabled me to get enrolled. However, I had to pay my whole tuition fee before I could take my final examination. Three days before the final examination, there was no way where I can borrow any money to complete the payment of my tuition. The stress and worry were almost unbearable. I just kept praying in my mind "Lord, will I be able to take my final exam or not? Please Lord, You know I can not pursue my plan unless you help me." After so many tears the previous night, a stranger pat on my back in the following morning and asked me if I am ready to take my final exam. I told him that I am ready, but I can not take it because I haven't paid my tuition in full. "How much more do you need?" I only need 2 hundred pesos to pay off my tuition. I have two hundred and fifty pesos for you and please don't ever think of paying me back!" The ecstasy, the joy and the relief overwhelmed me. I couldn't control the tears of joy flowing on my face. I like to embrace the stranger closed to my heart as an expression of my deep gratitude, but he left and disappeared so fast that I didn't even had the chance to recognize well his face. I only knew that God was truly helping me and He has not abandoned me. More and greater surprising helps have showered me in the coming years during my residency, my private practice and even during my retirement. God and Jesus Christ are truly the source of perfect blessings and hear the prayers of the faithful!

This book is dedicated to my children and relatives as well as to my readers to let them know of my background who, despite financial problem, can get their chosen education or vocation. In a country like USA where it is easy to get financial loan, the opportunity is tremendous. Nothing like this exists in the Philippines.

PART

1

1.

THE LONG JOURNEY OF A POOR FARM BOY TO BE A SURGEON AT ROANE GENERAL HOSPITAL

I am the youngest in a family of seven children. There were three girls, and four boys. The boy two years older than me was Alberto, and the youngest girl, Pacita, was born between Alberto and me. Only Alberto and I were able to go to college, simply because our parents could not afford to send the elder siblings. Even in high school, students had to pay a tuition fee. All my elders or entire family were farmers and by the time I was nine years old, the two elder brothers were already married and had their own families. So, Alberto and I were left helping our father farm our 4 acres, which was our source of livelihood. Being the youngest, my main duty during the planting season was to feed the carabao, which was used to plow and harrow the fields in preparation for planting rice, corn, or any other vegetable. The farm was well irrigated and we were able to plant rice twice a year. Nowadays, the farmers have an early variety of rice seeds so that they can plant and harvest three times yearly. Whatever was left over from our food supply was sold to buy our other needs.

In December 1942, the Second World War broke out and the Japanese occupied the Philippines for four years. Before the Japanese Army reached our home, we evacuated to the farthest mountain so that the soldiers would not find us, as we feared for our lives. Life was very hard and we never had enough food and other necessities. Fortunately, a year after occupancy by the Japanese Army, peace was restored. The Japanese encouraged the schools to reopen and they included Nippongo (Japanese Language) in the curriculum. Local administrative officers were reinstated. The Japanese were very friendly, and they taught us how to sing their national anthem. During the entire four years that the Japanese occupied the Philippines, I never went to school. For no reason, I simply lacked the interest. I just stayed home helping my parents doing light works at home. Because a platoon of Japanese soldiers occupied my brother's house by the side of ours, I played with them and learned to speak a little bit of their language. I was in fifth grade when the war reached the Philippines.

In 1945 the American Army liberated my homeland; the old regime was reestablished. The Japanese language was removed from the school system, and their national anthem was no longer sung. I was eager to return to school, and entered the sixth grade. One year later, I was admitted into my first year of high school.

We did not have a high school building from 1946 to 1947. My classes were held on the basements of people who owned large houses. Because of the urgent need to have school buildings, the people in the community were asked to donate their labor and materials to build rooms adequate to accommodate the first-year students. Anticipating the need for space for all the current and the coming higher school grades, the community constructed a larger building to accommodate all four grade levels. During the construction of the facility the town suffered through typhoons and flooding, which destroyed the fragile school building. However, the community rallied together to design bigger and stronger buildings. The students went from house to house, asking the people to find their generosity to donate to our educational building construction. Eventually, the building was constructed well, with rooms for all four grade levels. We even had additional buildings to hone our horticulture skills, as well as a space to raise poultry and swine. I was involved in not only ROTC (a requirement) but also with the vocational classes such as carpentry, agronomy, and the previously listed raising of poultry and swine. As the carpentry students added additional buildings the school grew to a greater size, adding in both space and facility.

As I grew older, I found the farming life to be a difficult one. My routine consisted of planting, harvesting, plowing the fields, and providing feeds for the working carabao,

My father also invested in two horses and a caratela (cart)large enough for my father to bring seven passengers with their crops. This business of transporting the farmers with their crops provided a source of additional income. In those early days, people did not own cars or jeeps to travel from one town to another. My workload increased with this additional business, and I had to cut grass between rice paddies every afternoon after my school classes. I increasingly found myself busy; my day did not end with the commencement of classes. I was always outside working in the farm, or in the yard and cleaning the stables. It was not an easy life, but it was an honest and hardworking living in the years following the Second World War.

During my high school, my brother Alberto and I raised poultry. We incubated 170 white- leg- horn eggs which were all successfully hatched. We constructed a 30 by 30 feet house for the chicks made of bamboo slabs roofed with a special long grass called Lidda. We vaccinated them with anti-Avian vaccine and learned to caponize the young roosters, (Cockerell). We fed them rice and corn raised from our farm.

During my second year of high school, I began to seriously contemplate what my future may hold. I did not see any good fortune in farming. Using my body every day was like tormenting each of my muscles, as I woke up aching every morning. But college seemed out of question, I could barely pay my tuition in high school. I had to raise two to three piglets and sold them every six or eight months old just to cover my tuition. During my senior year of high school, I found myself thinking about college often. Where can I get money to pay college expenses? Who is going to help my father with farming? I knew that only a miracle and the gracious assistance of the Almighty God could help me. Inspired by that thought, I set out to make the best grades I could achieve in hopes of earning a scholarship. I studied harder and sought to read any book I could hold my hands on. I was inspired by biographies of successful people such as Abraham Lincoln, General Arthur McArthur, Benjamin Franklin, and Dr. Frank Slaughter. I also read about crimes, and how lawyers defended their clients. The book "The Trial of Leopold and Loeb" authored by Clarence Darrow, their lawyer, fascinated me, and his miraculous success to save their lives held a special place in my mind. I also found myself reading speeches of famous people, including the great speeches given by Presidents of the United States. However, my favorite readings in my Bible impacted me in a much more powerful way. The Bible had become my rock. I had read the Bible since my second year in high school, and during my 4th year in high school, I read it more seriously trying to find words of God that will strengthen me. Indeed, I found inspiring scriptures stories to be very valuable and helpful. These several scriptures inspired me, and has truly compelled me to go to college and study about Medicine. The thought that human beings are created in the image of God, and are endowed with incredible talents had a monumental impact on me. "That with men this is impossible, but with God all things are possible." (Matthew 19:26)

John 15:17 states "If you abide in me and my words abide in you, ask whatever you wish, and it will be done for you." Other promises of Christ are found in John 14:11-14-"I will do what ever you ask in my name so that the Father maybe glorified in the son." "If in my name you ask for anything, I will do it." Matthew 21:22 -"Whatever you ask for in prayer with faith you will receive." Philippians 4:13-"I can do all things through Christ who strengthen me." "Commit your works to God and He will establish your plan." Proverbs kept trusting the Lord as it says, "Trust in the Lord with all your heart, and lean not in your own understanding; In all your ways acknowledge Him, and He shall direct your path." These verses became my inspiration, and compelled me to go to college and study medicine. I felt certain that God was calling me to become a doctor.

Before my college dreams could become a reality, my older brother Alberto was able to go first. He graduated with the highest-grade point average in his high school senior class. He was a very motivated individual, and never believed that poverty was a hindrance in getting a college degree. Alberto went to Manila and lived with a cousin who was the manager of the dietary department in the Manila Hotel. Alberto was able to obtain a job washing dishes during the day and went to college at night. After six years of immensely hard work, Alberto graduated with his law degree and went on to become a successful lawyer. His career was a commendable one, and he was eventually promoted to become a member of the Supreme Court, after several stops of serving as a judge. However, shortly before his appointment he was mercilessly murdered, snatched away from his promising life.

Alberto's death had an immense impact upon my life. I felt like I lost my other half; we were as close as brothers could be. We loved each other very much. In our earlier years we aspired to become lawyers, and we practiced debating while we worked in the field together. I would always ask him about college, and to make sure he saved his textbooks for me. When he learned of my intention to study medicine, he fully supported me. He encouraged me to become a doctor, because we needed a doctor for the family and the community. He always told me I would become a great doctor, and save many lives. His words struck me very deeply. I began to look at the potential a doctor would have for the community. Indeed, I found many people dying of diseases, suffering from lack of proper medical attention and inability to see a doctor due to poverty.

However, my doubts about going to college remained somewhat troubling in my mind. How can I truly study medicine when it is the longest and most expensive course to complete? I would not be able to work as Alberto did, for to be a student of medicine I would have to be a full-time student. I prayed every night, asking God if medicine was the correct choice. I finally concluded that to be able to heal the sick would be the best choice. I could not think of anything more important than to be a healer, a person who would help overcome an illness that could not combat on their own. Also, Jesus Christ Himself was an exceptional healer, curing people of diseases and lameness everywhere he traveled.

In anticipation of college, I raised three piglets six months before classes began and sold them the last week of May. My father chipped in a few pesos for my journey, and I picked out some decent clothes. With the blessing of my parents, I bid farewell to my family and boarded a bus headed towards Manila. The evening before I left, my brother Catalino sponsored a party where all the relatives, friends and all the neighbors came to bid me goodbye. The party was both lonesome but a few inspirational speeches finally turned to a joyful party.

After a six-hour bus ride, I arrived in Quiapo. Quiapo is the center of Manila, which is the old capital city of the Philippines. Suddenly,

I felt overwhelmed and felt lost. I did not know where to go; buses were leaving and passing in every direction. After a few minutes of confusion, I found a bus brazened with the logo UP (University of Philippines). I boarded the bus, and told the driver where I could be dropped to apply for admission in the medical field. I was told this was the correct bus, and after forty- minute bus ride it reached the school campus. I followed the other students to an office building and saw other aspiring teenagers registering. A receptionist saw me looking around, and asked if I had signed up for ROTC. When I responded I had not, she pointed to another building where to register. Tired and hungry, I carried my luggage a quarter of a mile to the ROTC building.

2

FIRST TWO YEARS IN COLLEGE, UNIVERSITY OF THE PHILIPPINES

Upon arriving in the building, a cadet in uniform told me to register with the other cadet sitting at a table. However, I stood there befuddled, because I had to pass through beneath the ten chairs he was pointing. To cross the room, I would have to pass under those chairs. He told me "this is not about hazing or punishing; all freshmen have to do it as a routine. So, don't be scared." After reaching the cadet on the other side, I filled my information on a sheet he provided; and the cadet informed me that I would have to return tomorrow morning for orientation. Afterwards, I returned to the registrar's office and joined the throng of other applicants. Luck was with me, as I happened to fall in line beside a gentleman who spoke the same local dialect I did. He informed me of the subjects we would have to take, and where he was from, and where he was staying. I told him I had just arrived from my province, and I had no place to reside. I then asked if there was any way I could stay with him. He replied "I would love to have you, but it would be my mother's decision. After registration you and I go home together to see my place, and my mother."

When I reached the receptionist, I told her I would like to register for the two-year premed course. She directed me to the next table. The next receptionist asked to see my high school diploma, and after she saw my grades she informed me I was qualified for the two-year premed program. She showed me which subjects to take for the upcoming semester, and she also told me about how to pay my tuition. I had to pay my full tuition cost by the final examination, yet I only had enough money to afford my books, ROTC uniform, lodging, and half of my tuition.

After registration, the problem of paying my tuition was heavy on my mind. However, the kind gentleman I had met in-line was offering to bring me to his mother's place, and it was an offer I could not refuse. The house was small, but I would have been delighted with a space in the floor, let alone a whole room to myself! The mother was very nice, and she informed me of the chores I would have to complete to earn my place. I thanked her many times over, delighted in my good fortune to find such a nice family and their willingness to take in a stranger.

After settling in with my housemates, I delved into my college courses. The professors were very strict, a start contrast with my high school teachers. We had to read the entire textbooks for our classes, and on any given day each classmate was expected to answer question fired by the professor. There were many subjects, and I consistently found myself struggling to find time to keep up in all my courses. Also, the freshmen had to report to ROTC every Saturday morning and took part in the activities located there, further cutting in my study time.

Despite the increasing difficulty of my college courses, a presiding problem consumed my daily thoughts. As the end of the semester approached, my final examinations were right around the corner. However, I still neither had the funds to pay my whole tuition, nor did I know anybody who could loan the money. Two days before the examination day, I was walking towards the university when a nice fellow I had never seen before asked if I was ready for my final. I told him I was, but I did not have an adequate amount of money to pay my tuition. He replied "How much do you need?" I told him I only need two hundred pesos to cover my tuition costs. The nice fellow answered in a generous tone "I have two hundred and fifty pesos to give you now and don't ever think of paying me back. Get ready and take the final exam in the morning." What a relief! The joy was overwhelming and I could only tell him, he is God's gift sent to me! I thanked him many times, and could not believe my good fortune! I wanted to embrace him close to my heart, but turned away fast and disappeared. May God bless him more!

The first semester, there were around two thousand premed students enrolled. In each of the subsequent semester, that number tallied off by roughly five hundred students. By the end of my fourth semester, the number of premed students had dwindled to around two hundred and fifty. At this time, only one hundred and twenty students were accepted by the college of medicine in the University of the Philippines. The application process would be one that provided serious implications to my future in medicine. However, I found myself no longer struggling to pay my end of the semester fees. During school breaks, I would return to my village and work, earning money to pay my tuition. While I was working often, and finding little free time, I was doing what I had always wanted to; succeeding in college and being well on my way to become a doctor.

3

MY YEARS IN MANILA CENTRAL UNIVERSITY

In the Philippines, after the 1950s, there were only four universities with college of medicine after the University of the Philippines, the University of Santo Thomas, and the Manila Central University. Manila Central University was closer; therefore I transferred there after my two years of premed ended. Only a dozen or so of my classmates at UP went to Manila Central, the others attended Far Eastern University (which was in its inaugural year of its college of medicine.) I chose the MCU College of medicine because it was a well established institution that had its own hospital. I was also able to rent a four bedroom apartment with three friends; we had agreed to split the costs of the apartment rent, utilities, foods and other expenses. Even better, the apartment was only a mere twenty minutes ride to the college. We even had enough leftover money to hire a maid to help us clean and cook, who did a fabulous job taking care of us.

Manila Central University was a small college that only had a few different buildings. The colleges of medicine and nursing were the only buildings that were on campus, besides the hospital. The students came from every reach of the Philippines, and there were even few of Chinese origin. There was a total of two hundred and twenty medical students enrolled in the first semester. The subjects were deep and riveting every step of the way. In my first year, I took anatomy, histology microscopic anatomy human physiology, biochemistry, and human cadaver dissection. The second year included courses on bacteriology, parasitology, microscopic pathology, pharmacology, diagnostic laboratory, physical examination, and the format of prescription. The third year was focused on medicine, therapeutics, ophthalmology, surgery, pediatrics, obstetrics, and gynecology. The fourth year consisted largely of patient history, physical examination, diagnosis, and management and hospital work. The fifth and final year at MCU was a rotation to different departments, focusing mainly on hospital work. This year was considered an internship; a way to gain experience before entering the field. The students would work at the campus hospital, but would also rotate to other nearby hospitals such as the Maternity and Children's Hospital and at North General Hospital to do minor surgery.

My personal experience with MCU was wonderful. I stayed as concentrated and focused as I could, and was rewarded for my efforts with high grades in each of my subjects. Money was no longer an issue, as I had become friends with people who came from a privileged background. These friends would take me out to eat to our favorite restaurant almost every evening after classes. And they took me to various sporting events and social gatherings. In return for their generosity, I would tutor them in any subject they required assistance. For some reasons, I was always elected in various leadership position in the medical campus including 2 different fraternities. However, despite all the good times I had at MCU my time there was concluding. At the end of the internship, the graduating students would choose which career path they would take. Some passed a medical board exam to start their own private practice. Others sought to be employed by a hospital or took a specialty residency program. I did not pursue these career paths; as I returned home to begin a private charity practice.

This was my solemn commitment to the good Lord and to express my gratitude believing that He was responsible for my becoming a doctor. These good people from my community had supported me every step of the way, and I was ready to give back in the only way I knew how; healing those who had watched me grow from a poor farm boy into a full-time doctor.

4

MY PRIVATE
MEDICAL PRACTICE

Even before the result on my board examination, I had started my own charity practice. I opened up an office in the basement of my sister's house, which was conveniently located across the street from the only market in town. This was an advantageous location because it allowed easy access to anyone who sought my help. During my internship I had gone with my classmates to drug companies to obtain samples to give away for my future patients. We were allowed to keep these samples, and use them if they were in no danger of expiring. These samples proved vital to my charity practice, and I had stored a substantial amount of these samples by the time I graduated. I was skilled in the area of prescribing medicine, and I made use of my skills. I treated people free of charge, doing what I could to improve their health. My professors at MCU tried to convince me to stay and specialize in general surgery, but I had a commitment to God and to my people to go home and help the sick people in my community. I truly believed that the gracious Lord was the responsible power who made it possible for guiding me to choose medicine, and to use my talent to heal others.

My private charity practice warmed my heart, I enjoyed working it. I saw sixty patients in my first day, when the flu season was in full swing. Most of them had an upper respiratory tract infection, but I did encounter a few cases of pneumonia. I would treat the pneumonia through an antibiotic IV, and would run follow up checks on them the next day. I did not have a car to drive, but I traveled around town on my bike. I enjoyed this practice immensely; I developed many good relationships with my patients. These patients would bring me fruits, vegetables, eggs, chickens, and fish in exchange for my free services. On my first few days after starting my practice, I saw many of my sick patients improve almost immediately. I felt like a true doctor, one that healed people. My practice reminded me of Jesus Christ's healing ministry, and I continued to be blessed by my Lord and Savior. None of this would have been possible if He allowed me to succumb to the pressures of not having the funds to pay my college tuition.

Every weekend that I was not busy with my practice, I visited a different towns and continued charity work. Reminiscent to my experience in my own community, I started to develop bonds with these patients in neighboring towns. They treated me like a close family friend, and I returned their affection with my own. In my own community, my former high school teachers took notice of my success and asked me to be the commencement speaker in the high school graduation. I found myself speaking as an honorary guest often, and I enjoyed myself very much. However, I was seeing problems that were irreparable by my efforts. I was not a qualified surgeon, and I sought to help them, but I could not. After three years of enjoying my charitable practice, I decided to come to the United States of America to specialize in surgery.

5

MY EXPERIENCE AT SAINT MARY'S HOSPITAL

I wrote to ten hospitals in the United States, searching for an internship or residency in surgery. I finally made the choice to apply at Saint Mary's Hospital in Niagara Falls, New York. A movie I had watched in high school showed Niagara Falls in its entire splendor, with the beautiful falls and stunning surrounding background. I had married recently, and concluded that Niagara Falls would be a wonderful location to honeymoon. But again, money played a major factor into my decision. I wanted to continue to learn the most in America, but I lacked the funds for transportation. After several agonizing days, I received a letter from Sister Agnes Ann, the acting director of the hospital. Expecting rejection, I opened the letter without much hope. Instead of a rejection, her letter contained a plane ticket from the Manila Airport, Philippines to the Buffalo Airport in New York! After landing, I was to meet a driver with a limousine who then drove me to the hospital in Niagara Falls. I was beyond shocked and overwhelmed with joy, and my family shared my bountiful optimism. A party was coordinated in my honor, and it was revered with a mixture of happiness and worries among my patients. They stressed to me how much I would be missed, but understood that the opportunity was not one I could turn down.

The following day I departed from Manila and boarded a plane to Honolulu, Hawaii. I had to wait a day to board my next plane, and I had arranged to meet with my cousins in Hawaii. I enjoyed their friendly accommodations for a day, and then continued on my journey. Next stop was in Los Angeles, where again I had arranged to meet with more cousins in the area. After spending another lovely night with relatives, my journey commenced once again. I left Los Angeles with my sights set on New York. When I finally arrived at Buffalo Airport, the driver of the limousine immediately recognized me and took me to the beautiful car with one luggage. I had never seen such a long and beautiful car in my life! I only thought how someone with so few things as I could warrant such a glamorous means of transportation! America was so different from the Philippines! I could drop a coin into a machine and it would dispense drinks or food. Nothing was like this in the Philippines! However, only time would tell the truth about life in America.

I arrived at St. Mary's Hospital around ten o'clock that morning. Sister Agnes Ann met with me, and took me to a tour on the hospital to learn the layout and meet some of the staff. As the tour concluded, Sister Agnes Ann informed me that my room was not quite ready, and that I would stay in the Bishop's room for a week. When I entered the Bishop's bedroom, I immediately felt overwhelmed. The room was beautiful, with an enormously large bed and comfortable furnishings. The next morning I told Sister Agnes Ann that I felt unworthy of residing in such a luxurious room, and I would be content with a regularly accommodated room and regular bed. Sister Agnes Ann replied with a loving voice, "Please never complain; while you stay in this hospital, I want you to enjoy your time here. This is the least we can do for you." I spent the rest of my day acquainting with the staffs and other interns, and further familiarizing myself with the layout of the hospital. When I inquired Sister Agnes Ann on when I would begin to work she told me this was my welcome week and that I would only join the daily morning rounds with the interns every day.

During the next week, I began to settle nicely in my new home. My room was finally ready, and I gratefully moved out of the Bishop's chamber. The intern's quarter was very nice. Each intern has a spacious room with a table and chair. There was a small room where milk bread and fruits were available. The living room or social hall was spacious and has a television and a radio. There were four bathrooms with each commode. The place was cleaned every day. All towels, bed sheets were changed every day. The hospital staffs were very friendly, and my fellow interns were extraordinary people. The interns and I developed a special bond. We became close friends very quickly; the eight of us became a great team. They were from every reach of the world; two from Ireland, two from Argentina, one from Canada, one from Lebanon, and one from Mexico. We spent all of our time together, whether on duty or not. I even cut their hair for a small fee on the weekends! The only time there was strife among the interns was schedule disputes, but we quickly dispatched that problem by conferring with Sister Agnes Ann and working out the differences.

Not only were my fellow interns delightful, the teaching program was also excellent. WE had different staff workers every month, and they thoroughly taught us what we needed to know. We had presentation every afternoon of interesting cases on the floor and discussed it very thoroughly, mentioning the differential diagnosis with the corresponding laboratory findings to arrive at correct diagnosis. There was also a diagnostic X-ray box with film and each intern was asked to write the diagnosis and dropped the paper into a slip- box where the assigned intern picked it out and then mentioned the x-ray findings in our afternoon rounds. During our rotation through the pediatrics section, we went to the famous Buffalo Children's Hospital and witnessed their clinico-pathological conference. The case was discussed heavily among the staff and the interns. There was one doctor assigned to do research on the latest management and another one to give the history of the disease. The pathologist discussed the case for the different diagnosis and the interns and attendants learned very well from the discussion. It was very educational and invaluable experience to all of us.

The surgical staff took us to make rounds on the surgical floor at Buffalo General Hospital, where we discussed interesting cases. Dr. Mallo, the surgical doctor, had a patient who complained of constipation and told him that at times he did not have bowel movement for about three to four days. The day before our round Dr. Mallo ordered a tablespoon of castor oil. Dr. Mallo had his patient took this, and the patient's health immediately improved. All of us interns were impressed, and we were pleased that he was happy with his medication. Dr. Mallo showed interest in teaching us. He even gave me as a gift, an Atlas of Surgical Textbook, where I learned how to perform common surgical procedures.

My wife arrived in the month of October, in 1961. She was tied up in her job in the Philippines as director of the Department of Science, at Christian University which delayed her move to the United States. She had previously earned a master's degree at Syracuse University; and earned additional units towards a PhD at Strong Memorial Hospital where she was culturing human tissues and did research work on the effects of cortisone in the chicken embryo. She came back to the Philippines to work as director of the science department at Christian University.

Sister Agnes Ann rented a house across the street from the hospital for my wife and me. The house was furnished with cooking utilities, television, radio, and even gave us all daily soaps, blankets, and towels. Sister Agnes Ann even provided my wife, Phoebe, with a job as a transcriber in the medical record department.

Before my wife arrived, I went to see the magnificent Niagara Falls on my weekends off and was surprised to always meet some Filipinos touring the area. The Canadian side of the Falls has also beautiful landscaped with beautiful flowers.

Everything went very well at Saint Mary's. The more I learned, the more I found myself how little I knew when I was an intern in the Philippines. Having repeated my internship in this hospital gave me so much confidence feeling like an expert in family medicine, learning how to read an EKG and chest x-rays as well as interpreting results of all blood tests. It was a great experience, in an environment full of positive people. Our social life was spent mostly associating with other Filipinos who were having their internship at Niagara Memorial Hospital. There was party whenever there was a birthday celebration. Christmas parties were always joyful with the exchanges of gifts and lots of Philippine delicacies.

However, my year as an intern was coming to an end. I would have to search for surgical residency and increase my knowledge in other fields of medicine. As the time to leave approached, Phoebe and I wished the great people of Saint Mary's good luck in their future endeavors. Sister Agnes Ann insisted that we take the furniture from the house with us, but we refused, neither have the means of transportation nor the desire to take them. We bid our farewell and continued our journey, wondering where God would lead us to next.

6

MY SEARCH FOR
SURGICAL RESIDENCY

My search took me to Rochester, New York, in hopes of finding surgical residency. I was told that if I wanted to be the best surgeon I could be, I should apply to Rochester General Hospital. I went to the hospital, and was impressed by the number of scheduled cases per day. There were roughly five hundred cases that I saw in the operating schedule, but this also included minor surgeries. There were only twelve residents working all on these surgeries, and I felt I would be overwhelmed if I worked here. I continued my search, and found myself at the Strong Memorial Hospital. The attending staff was the ones who perform the surgery; therefore I look for another destination.

Eventually, my search carried over to Flushing, at the Booth Memorial Hospital. I found out that all the residents were Filipinos, and I immediately felt at home. They were very relaxed and friendly, and welcomed me in with open arms. I decided to apply here, and I proceeded to show the director of surgery my credentials and recommendations. I was given residency, and I accepted the position.

There were three first year residents, two second year residents, and one chief resident. They only had three year programs but after serving as chief resident one would be considered a well-trained surgeon after having done all of the procedures for a general surgeon's program. The chief resident easily can perform more than 500 major surgeries in the hospital; because he did 3 major cases scheduled every day. And the residents did all the procedures. The attending staff served as our assistant in every case except in minor cases such as T&A (Tonsillectomy and adenoidectomy) which a first year resident usually did 5 cases every Friday when all the major cases were done. This was part of a first year case activity along with hemorroidectomy, breast biopsies, repair of inguinal hernias and excision of skin lesions. He also did fracture reduction and application of cast and read x-ray results and follow-up if the patient did not have a private physician.

I truly enjoyed my residency at Booth Memorial Hospital. I was always busy. I started making rounds on my patients at 6:30 AM, writing progress notes, changing dressings as needed, removing the stitches and writing discharge notes and may go home after they see the attending who arranged for the follow up. My first year was also very busy as we did not have intern rotating in the program. I had to write all the history and performed the physical examination of each patient on my floor. On top of that, I also attended to all the patients who came into the emergency room with lacerations and fractured bones. If I could not handle the case, I would require the senior resident's assistance. My first year also consisted of assisting on all major surgeries, doing breast biopsies, radical excision of hemorrhoids, fixing inguinal hernias, joining rounds with my seniors examining x-rays, and looking over the results of laboratory tests. On Friday afternoon, after our major surgical cases, I usually did five cases of Tonsillectomy and adenoidectomy (T&A). We had surgical rounds with the assigned attending staff every afternoon on all the peculiar cases. On Saturdays, we also had journal club presentations, which meant a resident had to present two or three cases that were published in a surgical journal. Once a month, we also had clinical-pathological conferences where other interesting cases were discussed. Most attending staff members and all the residents attended the meetings. We also had a one-hour pathological presentation by the pathologist every Wednesday afternoon on the operated cases that drew the most attention.

In the second year, the residents began a more in-depth cases of surgery. We were qualified to do more procedures, such as colon resection, exploratory laparotomy, breast lumpectomy, cholecystectomy, varicose vein stripping, and multiple excisions of the tributaries (branches). We also assisted in radical breast mastectomy, thyroidectomy, partial gastrectomy, abdomino-perineal resection (the removal of the lower colon, rectum and anus and creating a permanent colostomy). We also treated traumatic injuries to the abdomen, and repaired all torn tissues in the abdominal organs.

By the time our third year arrived, the residents had achieved the position of chief resident. The chief resident is not only expected to do all of the tasks the first and second years perform, but were expected to educate the younger residents and making the schedules. The chief resident was on call twenty- four hours for any problem that could arise, and were to be available at the drop of a hat in case a second year resident encountered an emergency problem he was not qualified to handle. Since my first year, I developed good relationship not only to our surgical staffs, but also to the OBGYN, orthopedists and plastic surgeons. I was grateful that they welcome me to scrub on their hysterectomies, C-section (cesarean) sections and hip pining. I learned to do all these procedures and anticipated having to do these procedures in the near future in my private practice. A chief resident was expected to perform roughly five hundred major procedures. In my experience as chief resident, I volunteered to scrub and assisted in many major operations, such as hysterectomy, Cesarean section, anterior and posterior repair, tubal ligation, or partial salphingectomy for sterilization and reanastomosis in the future should the patient decides to be fertile again. I help did a few hip pinning, for intertrochanteric fracture of the hip and even assisted plastic surgery. Much was required from the chief resident! I also found myself assisting in prostatectomy, partial nephrectomy, and vascular procedures. My knowledge had increased immensely in these three years! These experiences working beyond general surgery served me well in my later years, when I worked at hospitals not as advanced as Booth Memorial. It is noteworthy to mention that we had an excellent dog laboratory where we practiced doing different surgical procedures that was why we were able to do major procedures by the second year. By the end of my time at Booth Memorial, I was regularly doing many of the procedures the doctors could do, and I was doing them well! At the end of my three years, the director in charge of the residents handed me a plaque of excellent performance; proverbially thanking for my contributions as a resident. The plaque came with a check worth five hundred dollars, and the nursing department gave me a Bulova watch as a gift which I wear even today. What a blessing! God was so good, in so many ways! Because of the excellent programs at Booth Memorial Hospital, it was eventually turned into a New York University Medical Center, Flushing Division, New York with more departments added over the years, and now have a 5-year surgical program.

7.

My Experience at Guthrie Clinic/Robert Parker Hospital, Sayre, Pennsylvania

After my time at Booth Memorial, I was qualified to receive a job in general surgery. I applied to Robert Parker Hospital, and I was fortunate enough to be accepted. Robert Parker was in Pennsylvania, in a city called Sayre. The hospital was larger than Booth Memorial, and the attending staff did much more difficult procedures; which in turn allowed me to gain further operating experience. My main duties were to assist in the operation on the major surgeries, but they often had me perform the procedure myself. The staff at Robert Parker was impressed with my performance and knowledge, and I found myself increasingly doing more surgeries as the days rolled by. Not only was the number of procedures I was performing increased, I also had to keep up with my research. I worked on a variety of projects, including work on a surgical glove lotion with antibiotics incorporated. While I was very busy, I found time to admire Dr. William Sewell, a vascular surgeon who did the cardiac revascularization procedure. He had practiced the procedure over nine hundred times on dogs, and I was fortunate to be around a pioneering surgeon in the medical field. I was lucky to rotate working with him for three months, and he taught me how to perform selective arteriogram. We did coronary arteriogram in the morning, putting marks on the sites of partial obstruction caused by plaque, obtained a good picture; then in the afternoon, showed to the patient and proceeded to explain to the patient about the chances of them developing coronary heart disease or heart attacks. Some of the patients already had angina, a chest pain that occurs when an area of heart muscle does not receive a sufficient amount of oxygen-rich blood. In those times, few cardiologists could perform coronary arteriogram. Dr. Sewell was expert in doing selective arteriogram, and so as was the director of surgery. If a patient agreed to surgery, we would explain the procedure thoroughly, explaining all the benefits as well as the, complications; complete management, and follow up procedure. We used the internal mammary artery and intercostals arteries if needed to bypass the blockage with openings towards the end. About a centimeter length were created a few openings and we tunneled it into the heart muscle beyond the obstruction. The end of the bypass artery was sutured to the muscle of the heart so that it won't move out. The patient was given appropriate medications on discharge and be back on the tent day for a visit. Another coronary arteriogram is done after six months or earlier if chest pains occurred. Of course, the success rate (very high) as Dr. Sewell would always mentioned. The procedure itself was very complicated, and required many steps and the patience of a monk. I learned an extensive amount from Dr. Sewell. We did this procedure in 1967 when open heart surgeries were not done since artificial heart and lung machine were not available. Dr, Sewell also invented the snake procedure when the heart and lung machine were available. In this, he performed by taking a long saphenous vein hooked it around the heart making an opening beyond the obstructing plague.

I also assisted on cancer issues in the lungs, esophagus, and the kidneys and bladder. One of these cases I assisted was particularly very interesting in which the left renal artery showed an almost complete occlusion. The attendant examining the patient was shocked to find that the artery was entirely occluded throughout its length. Each time the surgeon clamped the artery, it fractured. There was nothing to be done to remove the plaque, except a bypass procedure. However, the patient passed away from her unique condition. The idea of a bypass catheter came into my mind, and I made a drawing like a Foley catheter, with an inflatable balloon on each end with different length and diameter. I contacted a lawyer, and I was able to obtain a patent in 1966.

At the end of my residency at Robert Parker Hospital, I was offered another chief residency, but I rejected the offer and informed the director that I was more interested in thoracic and cardiovascular surgery. Dr. Sewell and my director were kind enough to give me high marks and glowing recommendations. Again, I was continuing my journey to heal as many people as I possibly could. The good Lord had a plan for me, and I was eager to fulfill it.

8

MY ACCEPTANCE FOR RESIDENCY AT LONG ISLAND JEWISH HOSPITAL AT NEW HYDE PARK, LONG ISLAND, NEW YORK

Again fortune smiled upon me, as I was accepted for a two year residency in thoracic and cardiovascular surgery. My acceptance was pending approval of the Immigration office for additional stay in the USA since I first came with a student visa. Normally, when a student finishes his surgical training, he was supposed to return to his country and serve his people. Because of this, I had to present a letter of admission at Long Island Jewish Hospital before the Immigration Office extended my stay. The admission to a two-year approved program in such a specialized field was very competitive, and only two applicants were accepted. However, God's grace was apparent once again, as I was the first one chosen from a field of twenty five applicants.

The residents rotated for six months at Triburo Hospital, and we also worked at the Queens Hospital Center. Both hospitals were located in Queen, Jamaica, New York. At Triburo, the residents performed the pulmonary lesions, did open heart surgeries, and performed pacemaker insertion surgery. The Queen Hospital Center

29

held thousand beds, and it was always busy because it was a city hospital and services were practically free. At the Queens Hospital Center, I encountered patients with numerous different injuries; the emergency rooms were always very busy and all the seats were always full every hour of the day and night. Many traumas such as multiple fractured ribs and stab wounds were transferred to Triburo for chest tube insertion and observation and proceed to surgery if necessary. We had a gunshot wound that went through the heart muscles and the patient arrived at the emergency in shock. The patient showed to have tamponade, a situation when a large amount of blood is trapped within the pericardial sac limiting the full contraction of the heart as shown on the cardiogram where the height of the AVL segments are short. This requires an immediate release of the trapped blood before the heart stops beating. Hence, I made an incision on the left side of the heart, opened the Pericardium and suctioned out the blood that spilled in the lung cavity. We then proceeded to fix the lacerated cardiac muscles. And put chest drains. However, we found that there is evidence that the mitral valve was also damaged. So we went back the following day and fixed also the lacerated mitral valve. Needless to say, here at the emergency room or at Queens Hospital Center, we had a dynamic super talented trauma team, and when I arrived or notified of a serious injury, the patient already had IV, Foley catheter, x-rays and different blood tests are done and other vital signs, All I have to do was to read the x-rays, check all the results of the blood tests and available for transfusion, the electrolytes and talk with family either by phone or in person if they are around.

We also performed each of the pacemaker insertions for third degree AV block, and then transferred them back to Queens Hospital Center.

However, at Triburo the residents did several different kinds of pulmonary lesions for cancer and thoracoplasty for persistent large cavitation (due to chronic inflammation by tuberculosis). We did diagnostic bronchoscopy and neck and mediastinal lymph node biopsies for cancer in the lungs and esophageal lesions. The residents also performed open heart surgeries at Triburo Hospital. In those days CAT SCAN was not yet available. We read our own x-rays and make our own diagnosis and monitor our patients intensively whether they need surgery or not.

The first year residents had to prepare the patient by inserting the catheters, the artificial lung, IV fluids, and assisting the chief resident in any way possible. After the procedure, the first years wrote the post-operative orders and checked on the patient until discharge.

The chief resident was the second year resident, and he had the choice to do any of the procedures he was qualified to do. I enjoyed my second year as chief resident doing difficult surgeries, eager to expand my knowledge. The chief resident was responsible for attending all the consulting sessions, and helped the first year residents wrote the patient's history and outcome of examination. We reviewed and interpreted the x-rays, and ran tests in our laboratory. The residents were a very busy bunch at Triburo Hospital!

The next six months were devoted to Long Island Jewish Hospital, which had a five hundred bed capacity. The first year residents performed the same procedures here as they did at Triburo and Queens Hospital Center. Most of the private cases were worked by the attending staff, but many of the cases were performed by residents. The chief resident again had preference, and my second year, I earned as chief resident. I rarely wrote progress notes at this point; I was always busy working different cases attending consulted cases with first year or a 3rd year surgical resident rotating in our service. I dictated the laboratory tests, and outlined the procedures the residents would perform on the patients. My time spent as chief resident taught me about responsibility, and foreshadowed a portion of the strenuous life of a doctor.

As my time ended, I was facing yet another decision. Triburo had offered me to stay in the program to help teach incoming residents, but I politely declined. I neither had a permanent visa, nor a license in New York. I was again changing location, looking for a permanent residence to establish myself and my family. The director found it a few months later that if the hospital hiring me or employ me, I could work in the hospital as a teaching staff in the same way that I was sponsored while I worked in more than one hospital following my residency. I feel it was too late to go back as I enjoyed working on my own for a living especially my family is growing.

9

YEARS AFTER
RESIDENCY

During my senior year in thoracic surgical residency, I wrote to the Immigration Office and implored about changing my student visa into a permanent one. After applying, I received my permanent visa six months later. I still resided in Flushing at this time, and I got position as a house surgeon at the Hospital for Chronic Diseases in Bronx, New York. I only worked in this location for two months, and it served me like a refresher course for general surgery. My residency in thoracic surgery was limited to chest and blood vessels. In this location, I did cholecystectomy, hip pinning, setting fractures, and plastic surgery. I learned a lot in my time here, but it left me looking for more.

Towards the conclusion of my time at the Hospital for Chronic Diseases, I received a call from Holden Hospital in Logan, West Virginia. I had a former surgery resident who was in the area, and he gave my telephone number to the hospital, which was openly seeking surgeon. Later on, I visited Holden Hospital. I accepted the job here, and immediately found myself swamped with work. I was very busy at my new location, performed 3 surgeries in the morning and I routinely saw sixty patients in a single afternoon. I was able to see such a substantial number of patients because the hospital provided me with a nurse and technician. They helped me tremendously! I still had to write up patient's history and physical exams on all patients, but having a personal staff to assist was a blessing.

Many of the emergency cases were treated at Logan General Hospital, not Holden Hospital. Logan General had better facilities and much more equipped for extensive surgery. However, one time I had to perform an emergency case at Holden, which did not have the best resources for a surgery of this caliber. The patient was an eighteen year old, who was being treated for three months pregnancy. The patient had begun having extensive vaginal bleeding, and she checked into the hospital three hours after her symptoms appeared. Her attending doctor was on vacation, so I was called in to examine the patient. The exploratory findings were unusual; she had two ovaries that were bigger than the uterus that occupied the abdominal cavity. I had to remove both ovaries before I could even reach the womb. I opened the womb, and injected estrogen to initiate a strong contraction. I scraped all of the tumors present, but the bleeding continued. Eventually, I concluded I had to remove the womb to save the patient's life. She recovered after extensive surgery, and I asked her to follow up with me if she needed anything. Needless to say, it was one of the most strenuous and painful operations I ever had to perform. I worked in all 3 hospitals but did major cases in Logan General Hospital. The third hospital where I also work is/was Guyon Valley Hospital owned by Dr. Chilag about 3 blocks away from Logan General Hospital. Dr. Chilag was impressed about my efficiency to a variety of procedures and was not aware that I left Logan because the hospital board didn't approve an increase of my benefits. When Dr. Chirag learned that I came to work at Roane General Hospital, he called me and wrote me eagerly wanting me to go back to Logan, work at his Guyon Valley Hospital with a starting salary of $100,000.00. I rejected the offer, because my mind was not focus on getting rich, besides, I was the only one who applied at Roane General Hospital and has written all the policies, all the format of patient's records and summary discharges, also had the hospital bought all the necessary equipment needed for the emergency, office spaces and all the floor including the Skilled Nursing Facility. I could claim that I am the founder of the clinical part of the hospital. I taught the nurses in the operating room about the use of the different instruments, also taught Cardiac Resuscitation to all the nurses together with late Mrs. Barbara Camp. I volunteered as medical director to the SNF. I addition, I volunteered as the medical director of the Roane County Emergency Services with no pay. As the director, I kept update on the rules and handling patient's care. I called meeting once a month to discuss at least ten charts, to find out if the patient's care was appropriate. Since I had experienced many different injuries and their management, I enjoyed many challenges to work which sometimes require improvising any tool that I can use.

People cannot understand why I didn't buy the mansion house or many real states. Again, my thoughts were not focus on those things. Nevertheless, I bought a few rental apartments just to have my wife something to do. I think it is important for me to tell the world, that I even donated $30,000.00 out of my small guaranteed salary. Unfortunately, the Late Mr. Foster Hedges failed to give me a receipt.

Some people said that they never realized how fortunate they are to have me stayed in Spencer.

10

LIFE AT ROANE GENERAL HOSPITAL

Towards the end of 1969, (September) I came to visit a newly built hospital about to be finished in Spencer, West Virginia. It was a beautiful building, with spacious operating rooms. Mr. Robert Smith was in charged of the construction and was to be the new administrator. Mr. R. Smith also told me that he also helped in the construction of Jackson General Hospital in Ripley, WV and was the new administrator as well. Mr. Smith kept contacting me in the month of October and came to visit again. I met also the late Mr. Foster Hedges who was the chairman of the hospital board, and also the president of the First National Bank of Spencer. After I showed them my curriculum vitae, they eagerly wanted me to come to work and help them open in the new hospital. Mr. Hedges told me "that the hospital is the culmination of unstinted efforts of all the residents of Roane County and many other generous people and without you, the building is meaningless." I realized how vital my presence in the realization and fulfillment of their dreams and how wonderful it is to have well-trained doctors to provide excellent medical services to this small but wonderful community. I also found out that to open a new hospital, a surgeon is a requirement. I am humbled to say that I am that surgeon. The thoughts that these nice people truly need me have melted my heart and I could not say "No" despite the attractive financial offer by the owner of Guyan Valley Hospital in Logan. I accepted the position to start working on November 15, 1969 with a small guaranteed salary of $36,000.00 but whatever extra I make, will be added. At the end of the year, I made $76,000.00 and when the late Mr. Hedges asked about the extra $30,000.00 that I made, I humbly told him to be my donation to the hospital which was financially struggling then. I lived in one of the rooms on the first floor, while they continued to finish the building and I was provided with meals.

I could not find a nice suitable place for my growing family until June 1970. The house that I bought was small, but it was the ideal place. We added extra rooms to fit my 6 children.

I helped designed the rooms on the first floor near the emergency room. There were 3 rooms besides the larger room for emergency cases. One room will be my temporary office while the other 2 rooms were for examining patients.

I ordered all the equipment, examining tables, blood pressure, otoscopes, ophthalmoscope, sutures, gloves everything needed for pelvic examination in every room. I had the hospital bought all the equipment needed in the operating rooms as well as in the floor including a suction machine for chest problems and a few retractor and vascular clamps. I wrote all appropriate consents for every procedure including the side reactions of anesthesia with our nurse anesthetist. I chose the design for recording patient's history, summary discharges and others including those for the SNF to be consistent with the requirements for joint commission accreditation. The SNF was vital part of the hospital in order to be able to get some federal grants. I served as the medical director for the SNF as a free service including my position as medical director for the Roane County Emergency Squad until I retired after 30 years. As medical director of the SNF, we maintained a high level of medical care to all our patients and never had any deficiency. In the Roane Emergency Squad, I conducted monthly meetings with all members of the ER squad reviewing all the patients' record to make sure each patient was properly handled. I gave them lectures on early management of all injuries and critical medical problems. In addition, to the 3 months before the hospital opened, I taught with Mrs. Barbara Camp, other nurses hired, cardiac resuscitation for all the future employees. On the day that the hospital opened, we had a complete team and although bare, the personnel were very efficient. We had Marybelle Hersman as the director of Nursing and helped in all departments; Blondell Deem; Chestine Smith; Barbara Camp; Joan Burch; Some of the O.R. technicians included Alice Burdette, Mr. and Mrs., Lundy Holcomb. To complete my OR TEAM, I have to mention our special NURSE ANE STHETIS, DOLORES STIWART. She has excellent and pleasing attitudes, well expertise and very responsible. She was always on time whenever she is needed. Her presence enabled us to perform all surgeries that we did. Truly, a very valuable personnel. Over the years more nurses, other personnel and doctors joined the staffs. The nurses worked very hard; they went to the floor wherever they were needed. We had an active maternity as well as nursery for the newborn. Miss Anna-Neal Denbigh, now Anna-Neal Taylor, Joined the nursing staff and was in charge in the maternity ward. Dr. Pedro Lo joined me several days later and shared the offices in the emergency room. We helped each other in many major procedures. Other doctors on the staff included Dr. Richard Brown, A family physician, Dr. James DePue who owned a hospital, also a family physician and surgeon; Dr. Aaron Cottle also joined later. Soon we had Dr. Pedro and Erlinda Ambrosio an internist and pediatrician respectively. I knew Dr. Pedro Ambrosio before he came to Roane General because he trained at the Booth Memorial Hospital where he came after I finished my training and visited him in the BMH asking them to join me at Roane General Hospital. I was happy that they did and we all worked together. We soon have Dr. Cheng Hung, an OBGYN, and his wife Min Lin Liu, a board certified pediatrician. Then came Dr. Caroll Christiansen, a family physician, who had the privilege to take care of maternity patients. In those early days, we were very busy and we covered the emergency cases without additional fee from the hospital. Eventually, the hospital hired additional MDs to work in the emergency because it became very busy.

Shortly after the hospital opened, the hospital hired an architect to build another building which was and is now the Roane Medical Building which was finished within a year and my office moved to the building. Dr. Pedro Lo moved besides my office while the Ambrosios and the Hungs occupied two of the larger spaces in the office building.

I thoroughly enjoyed my practice in Spencer. We provided many wonderful services which extended as far as Calhoun County to Flatwoods to the North, Wirt County to the West, and Walton to Clendenin to the South. I did a lot of orthopedics including hip pinning for intertrochanteric fractures and long bones. My extra efforts in assisting and doing hysterectomy, C-section, anterior and posterior repair and other gynecologic procedures when I was a surgical resident at Booth Memorial have provided extra services to the community. These procedures not offered in many hospitals like CAMC (if you are a general surgery) became a teaching model for the other staffs.

It was a joy for me to contribute $30,000.00 at the end of 1970 at the time the hospital was always monthly short of operating fund.

11

MY CONTINUING MEDICAL EDUCATION

During those years of medical and surgical practice I enjoyed attending many famous medical centers like MGH at Harvard, Mayo Clinic in Rochester, Minnesota; Mount Sinai Hospital in New York, The Cleveland Clinic in Cleveland, Ohio, and The Philippine Surgical Society in America and many others just to learn the best that I could. I had to go for in- service training for the many uses of Endoscopic and laparoscopic procedures. I also attended yearly symposium on Bariatrics Medicine. I also joined many medical associations. I received my certificate for medical director after I took classes from the University of Minnesota in 1990, the 2nd MD in WV to be certified. I was recertified in 1996 following extensive educational hours sponsored by the American Medical Directors Association. I received four plaques one from the Fellow American College of International Physician at the New Orleans Symposium for outstanding achievement on May 11, 2001; one for most outstanding APPA(Association of Philippine Practitioners in America) Families given in Charleston in conjunction with the APPA 23rd Annual Convention on July 27-31

1994; one from the Tri-State Fil-AM Association for outstanding achievement given in Charleston and another one from the Philippine American Association of Family Physicians in Recognition for My Role and Accomplishments of my Family presented also in Charleston.

During my active practice, I was appointed an honorary faculty of College of Medicine, Marshall University and was in charge of residents rotating in surgery at Roane General Hospital.

A surgeon friend of mine at Clarksburg Medical Center asked me to join with him in the US Army Reserved and I did in February 1986 and was given the rank of Lt. Cornell, but I took an Honorary Discharge in late December 1989, just before the war in Iraq.(Jan 1990)

During my retirement, I served as member on the committee of policy making body, also board member of MID-OHIO Valley Health Department; member of the advisory committee of the License Practical Nursing Section Roane/Ripley Technical Center. My wife and I were an active volunteer- member of Mountain of Hope, a satellite of West Virginia Cancer Coalition Prevention and Control until her accident. She served in various capacities at the Memorial Church in Spencer till we joined the St. John Methodist Church. I served as Lay Leader at the Memorial church and delivered a few sermons just to learn to speak before a congregation.

I belong or member of the Moriah Lodge in Spencer; Scottish Rite of Free Masonry in Charleston and the BENI KEDEM SHRINERS in Charleston, part of Shriners International.

I play a few tunes on my violin and harmonica without knowing a single note. I recently learned how to play my Ukulele.

I am married to the former Phoebe Jose, who had a master's degree in Zoology at Syracuse University and earned additional units for a higher degree; and with whom we are blessed with 6 wonderful children who are now busy in their chosen profession.

I retired doing major surgery in April 2004 when malpractice insurance premium became excessively high. I did work in a clinic for 4 years and worked as medical director and staff in 3 nursing homes which I thoroughly enjoyed helping elderly patients. I retired working in the last facility; Nursing Home And Rehabilitation Center, in Ivydale, WV in 2007 at the age of 75.

As I contemplate humbly on this long and incredible journey, I could not have overcome the many insurmountable challenges without the energy, the persistent passion, the immense desire to help the sick and the patience bestowed upon me by the Almighty Power whom I am eternally grateful for all the many blessings also bestowed on my entire family especially to my wife and well disciplined children. As a medical and surgical doctor, I learned so much from my patients who presented many serious physical, mental and emotional problems and as a husband and father I credit the wisdom that I learned from my wife and my children.

12

LIFE DURING
RETIREMENT

I am fortunate to be healthy in the four dimensions of my life; physically, emotionally, mentally, and spiritually. I visit my doctors regularly for a complete physical checkup and complete laboratory exams. In December 2002, following a coronary arteriogram that showed 50% atherosclerotic plaque at 1 cm from the root of left coronary artery; I had one coronary bypass successfully with no significant postoperative pain that I never took any pain pill like Tylenol. I never had any symptom of angina before or after my surgery. The plaque was detected on a routine EKG and coronary arteriogram.

I developed acute pericarditis with effusion and a pericardiotomy was done to drain the fluid. I recovered from this, and have not encountered any major health issues. I developed this when I joined my nieces on a medical mission to the Philippine; where I labored strenuously doing surgery one after another in an extremely hot climate for seven hours. My nieces and I and 2 other surgeons in the Philippines performed roughly two hundred surgeries. Despite my uncomfortable circumstances, my desire to heal others gave us unforgettable joy and experiences. Every day, we performed all the operations and left no one unattended. Since then I have settled into my retired life. I enjoy spending time with my wife, and visiting my children as well as their children.

I spent my leisure time searching and reading many newly researched healthy supplements but not giving up my routine going to RGH GYM for a few minutes of exercise. I consider having a blessed and fortunate life. I have no regrets in not able to use my specialty in Thoracic Surgery and although my name is not written in the walls of the hospital, I thoroughly enjoyed my medical practice in Roane County where I found countless good people where my name is permanently engraved in their hearts and minds. In all the years that I have stayed in Roane County, I have some good stories which were published in a book," Great Prescriptions for Righteousness and Success". The same content of the book (hard Copy) in another title "Great Prescriptions to a Better YOU". I highly recommend that you buy the later title and is available at Amazon. Com. Or you may call 304-519-0112 and will be hand- delivered to you if you live in Spencer or I can mail it to you in your address.

It is my deep prayer that the Almighty Lord will continue to bless this country and her people. I will continue to study about human life through the Bible and medical science; keeping up with newly research breakthroughs in nutrition and supplements.

PART

2

13

MANAGING
THE MIND

I believe that it is very important to know ourselves not only the physical aspect, but also the emotional, mental and spiritual. Life doesn't only consist of the physical functions of all the parts of the human body. I believe there is much more beyond the capacity of the human body and that is our mind which is not totally the function of the brain. The mind has no anatomical identity, but it has many incredible capabilities. The mind and its function are one of the most important part of our life. I say this because it is the eternal fountain of our thoughts which represents our inner life. I believe that it is the governing body of our physical structure and the brain is the executor of our actions or the expression of our thoughts. Our mind is subject to various influences and they can be beneficial or lead to disaster depending upon its target or motive. Hence it can be positive or negative. Positive thoughts are beneficial and is based on love and Divine principles; while negative thoughts are based on worldly values such as greed, jealousy, arrogance, impatient, unrighteous, selfish, poor discipline to mention a few. It is therefore important that we learn to manage our mind in a way that our thoughts are positive and beneficial. Remember the verses in Philippians 4:8&9 "Finally brethren, whatsoever things are true, whatsoever things are honest, whatsoever things are just, whatsoever things are pure, whatsoever things are lovely, whatsoever things are of good report; If there be any virtue, and if there be any praise, think on these things. V9 These things which you have learned, and received and heard and seen in me, do and the God of peace shall be with you."

What is mind? Webster dictionary mention it as the conscious and mental events; the capabilities of an organism, the organized conscious and unconscious adaptive mental view. The Thesaurus simply states as the intellect, seat of consciousness, cognitive power. These definitions basically suggest the same meaning as those of the Webster dictionary. I like to think that mind is the seat of consciousness with cognitive power. I also like to think that it is spiritual in nature since thoughts are spiritual in nature and are powerful. Thoughts are invisible and indestructible as opposed to visible matter. Thoughts may fade away, but it can be recovered; while matter when destroyed, it is gone. One may make similar to it, but no longer the original matter. Thoughts are very fast even faster than the internet. Like the speed of a message you send from your country to another; while your thoughts take place in a split of a second. In the same manner, when you have seen the Grand Canyon before, it only takes a few second to appear in the screen of your mind while you are in Manila, Philippines. Again, if you have seen the Yellow Stone, or Butchart Garden in Canada, or the famous Rice Terraces in the Philippine, or the Chestine Chapel in the Vatican Square at Rome it only takes a second to appear in the screen of your mind.

As I mentioned earlier, the mind is subject to various influences depending upon the effect of your sensation. The unique and beautiful places mentioned above are the results of your visual sensation; and using your ears, you may enjoy the musical sounds of Ivanco or Barbara Streisand or the Mozart pieces which may create a healing balm; or the crying of a hungry baby, that arose your sympathy; and if you use your hands, you may feel the pulse of your beating heart, the rough surface of a sand paper or the intense heat of a burning steel. And so the mind has a negative or positive effect in the body. What you put and dwell in your mind is what you become. And so, if the thoughts are beautiful, noble and commendable, they bring beneficial effects in the mind and consequently in the body. If the thoughts are poor like thinking to steal, to murder, to be arrogant instead of being humble the outcome is very unhealthy. And so, like the food that you eat, if it is nutritious, your body may become healthy. But if not, although it may be delicious because it is filled with sugar or fat, you may develop obesity, diabetes or heart problem. As the Bible says, "As a man thinketh in his heart so is he."

Fear, anxiety, depression, loneliness or worries are the results of unhealthy thoughts. It takes a lot of education, experiences and education from books, from counselors, psychologist, and psychiatrist to be able to cope up on those stressful problems and be immune to all those situations. It takes a lot of discipline and self-control to do righteously on our daily activities. It is important and best to see a qualified doctor to seek help so that you may avoid chronic stress, unhappy life and to restore a joyful and vibrant life. I believe that there is always a better way to do things so as to bring harmony in one's life and to others. And so, we should analyze our attitudes, our habits, our thoughts, and write those that are unpleasant, unwholesome, unrighteous, and eliminate them. We should substitute and strengthen those that are pleasant, kind, gentle, peaceful, pure and loving thoughts which bring good relationship to oneself and to others.

There are diseases of the mind such as bipolar disorder, schizophrenia, Alzheimer's disease, Parkinson's Disease, ADHD to mention a few and these conditions are very difficult to treat or cure. In fact there is no known cure for Alzheimer's and Parkinson's disease. All these diseases are the outcome of brain damage leading to the malfunction of the mind and brain various other causes. All the current prescribed medications have failed to even relieve those conditions. They are all believe to be due to environmental factors, poor dietary intake with unhealthy additives, lack of exercise and lack of education and some are believing to be due to inherited DNA. Since the mind is partly a function of the brain, it is imperative that the brain be nourished with appropriate foods, such as the blue berries, omega 3s, phosphatidylserine, pyridoxine, magnesium, Coenzyme COQ10, folic acid, B12, PQQ (pyrroloquinoline Quinone), bio-curcumin, Quercetin, R-Lipoic acid, Acetyl L-Carnitine, Luteolin, Lecithin, DHA, vinpocetine and vitamin D3.

All those problems are difficult to treat but there are now newly researched supplements and proper dietary (those of the above intake that may relieve some of the symptoms of those illnesses.) Dr. Russell Blaylock and Dr. Mark Hyman are the experts I know who can deal these problems. I am sure you can find their names in the internet. Both of them are prominent authors along those lines. Dr. Daniel Amen is a neuroscientist and psychiatrist has written several books relating to the brain. Among the popular books he has are "Change Your Brain, Change Your Body; Magnificent Mind at Any Age; Making a Good Mind Great; Healing Anxiety and, Preventing Alzheimer's Disease; Depression; Healing the Hardware and the Soul and Healing ADD." I am sure there maybe others who are experts on the subjects.

There have been a few articles about the conscious mind and the subconscious mind. There is an even a term like super subconscious mind. I believe the later is the same as the subconscious mind. The conscious mind is basically the function of the brain. The activities are well planned and executed or that it starts first as thoughts then analyzed before it is executed. Subconscious mind on the other hand works automatic without even feeling what is happening such as digestion and absorption of foods; pumping of the heart to distribute all the nutrients of foods to all the cells of the body; the formation of urine; the various chemical reactions taking place in every cell, in the liver, in the bone, in the brain, in the spleen, in the intestine and the processing of memories; the active formation and destruction of cells in the skin, in the bones and in every organ in the body.

It seems like the subconscious mind is closely related to the Holy Spirit and as such, it is Spiritual and Divine and has much incredible power. Currently, I am reading two books; The first one is "Norvell's Mental Laws For Successful Leaving by Anthony Norvell and the second is Mind Power Into The First Century by John Kehoe" Both books are excellent and the one authored by John Kehoe was number 1 Best Seller. Both books are good not only inspirational but extremely educational because they tell us about the incredible but the minds, the Conscious Mind, The Subconscious Mind and the Master Mind or Universal Mind. There is much to learn about the incredible power of those minds and how to use them to improve one's life. I am trying to learn how to use the subconscious and the Universal Mind. Hoping that I maybe able to prove their teaching. I urge you to get those books and apply them to be the man you want to be.

THE
HOLY SPIRIT

In my search for excellence, it takes a lot of understanding about life; its origin, about analysis of oneself and its relationship to all living creatures on planet Earth not only to mankind but more especially to the Almighty and Omnipotent God Creator. To learn about the environment and everything that dwells on itself is a complicated science. But after all, beyond those many studies, only steadfast love and harmonious relationship among the dwellers can yield to peace, prosperity and a joyful life. It is fascinating that God planned our planet Earth to be His paradise kingdom, but after the creation of the first man and woman, Satan,(the devil snake) deceived them and ate the fruit which God forbid and will lead them to die. And so, as a punishment, the woman will have intensified labor pains and be dominated by her husband; while the snake will move on its belly and will eat dust all the days of its life. And so, some Christian- believers or they think we inherited the sin of disobedience. The consequence of sin in the Bible is death. But God loves us very much. He created us in His image with incredible talents and creativity and power to rule all the living creatures including those in the air and in the sea. In addition, He had the Bible written by chosen prophets and apostles so that we may know everything that He wants us to be. He had His teachings written in stone and emphasized us to follow faithfully. He even sent His son Jesus Christ, spiritually born in a human, to demonstrate to us that we can live as an abiding and faithful child; that we can live a much better life if we honestly and sincerely not only believe in God but by actually do believe in Christ, who advocated to Love GOD with all our heart, mind and strength and Love others as we love ourselves. That we can be forgiven of our shortcomings and tress passes if we confess our sins and reform to our best. What a truly magnificent love Christ and God have for us!

So what or who is the Holy Spirit? What does He do? How can we have it? And how can we harness His power so that we can achieve many seemingly impossible goals?

The Holy Spirit is the 3rd person in the trinity of God; God the Father, Jesus Christ, the son, and the Holy Spirit. The Holy Spirit is male in gender; he is also called the Advocate, the Comforter, the Helper and the spirit of Truth. The Spirit possesses Divine attributes;

* Omniscience ;(All –knowing) The Spirit searches all things, yea, the deep things of God (1Cor.2:10,11).
* Omnipresent (present everywhere) Whither I shall go from thy Spirit (Psa.139:7) The Spirit dwells at the same time in the hearts of all believers (John14:17)
* Omnipotence: (All powerful)"not by might nor by power, but my Spirit—(Zech.4:6). It is in fact the Spirit that creates. "The Spirit of God had made me (Job 33:4)
* The Truth-Jesus says, "I am the Truth," because He is God. In the same manner, in 1 John 5:6, the Spirit is declared to be the Truth.
* He is the Spirit of Life (Rom. 8:2) as God is the living God.
* He is the Spirit of Love (11Tim.1:7)
* The Holy Spirit is God Himself; the Lord is in the Spirit (11Cor.3:17)
* God is Spirit (John 4:24)
* To lie to the Spirit is to lie to God Himself (Acts 5: 4)
* The Holy Spirit teaches: "But the Helper, the Holy Spirit, whom the Father send in My name, He will teach you all

things, and bring to your remembrance all that I said to you."
John 14:26

* The Holy Spirit guides: "When the Holy Spirit, who is truth, comes, he shall guide you into all truth" John 16:13

* The Holy Spirit comforts;" I will ask the Father and He will give you another Comforter and He will never leave you; John 14:16

When did the Holy Spirit given to the human race?

John 14:16 "And I will pray the Father, and He shall give you another Comforter that He maybe with you forever.(John 16:7) "It is expedient for you that I go away: but if I go not away, the Comforter will not come upon you: but if I go, I will send Him unto you."

Acts 1:8 "But ye shall receive power when the Holy Ghost is come upon you; and ye shall be my witnesses. Acts 2: 38,39 "You shall receive the gift of the Holy Ghost. For to you is the promise, and to your children and to all that are afar off, even as many as the Lord, our God shall call unto him."

How do we receive the Holy Spirit?

Paul states in Galatians "Christ redeemed us from the curse of the law– that we may receive the promise of the Spirit through Faith ". It is not necessary to wait several days or months. The only requirement to receive the Holy Spirit is through faith in Jesus Christ.

What are the gifts of the Holy Spirit?

Read 1Cor. 12:4, 8-10, 28; Verse 8 gift of wisdom, knowledge; V9: gift of faith healing; V10: gift of working miracles, prophecy, discerning. The gift of tongues and interpretation, V28; gift of apostleship, teaching, giving assistance, of governing, evangelist and being pastor.(Eph.4:11)

The fruits of the Holy Spirit Galatians 5: love, joy, peace longsuffering, kindness, goodness, faithfulness, gentleness and self -control.

What are some of the works of the Holy Spirit besides those gifts and fruits? He reminds us about the teachings of Christ and to empower us in many aspects of our life and activities.

Acts 16:11-13-14 He is to convict the world about sin, about righteousness, and judgment. V13-He will guide you into all the truth, v14 He is to declare to you of what to come.

He is to remind us about the teachings of Christ; He is to guide us unto all the truth.

The Spirit Versus the Flesh

Acts 5:16-26 "Live by the Spirit, I say, and do not gratify the desires of the flesh. 17-For what the flesh desires is opposed to the Spirit and what Spirit desires is opposed to the flesh; for these are opposed to each other, to prevent you from doing what you want. 18-But if you are led by the Spirit, you are not subject to the law. 19-Now the works of the Spirit are obvious: fornication, impurity, licentiousness, 20-idolatry, sorcery, enmities, jealousy, strife, anger, quarrel, dissension, faction, 21-envy, drunkenness, Carousing and things like these. I am warning you as I warned you before: those who do such things will not inherit the kingdom of God. In short, the works of the Spirit are not only to remind us about the teachings of Christ and the Apostles, but encourage us to be totally obedient.

To be filled with the Holy Spirit is to have absolute faith to Christ and yield our whole life to Him, meaning every part of our being, our thoughts, our actions, our habits and our emotions. The slightest sin, consciously committed and not immediately confessed and abandoned, will lower the spiritual level. Straightway the Spirit ceases to occupy all and His living power no longer reveals itself as hitherto. It is obvious that a believer who is truly spiritual and filled with the Spirit will be more severely attacked by the adversary than a carnal Christian. The filling of the Holy Spirit is not forever. Once we grieved him and commit sin, He abandons us, but we can have Him back in the same way we received Him. When we are filled with the Holy Spirit, we are endowed with His gifts and fruits and live a wonderful life."

Note all the scriptures quoted above are from the New International Version.(King James)

The following verses quoted from the book of John are some of my favorite promises of Jesus Christ:

John 14:12,13, 14 "Very truly, I tell you, the ones who believe in me will also do the works that I do, and in fact, will do greater works than these, because I am going to the Father. 13- I will do whatever you ask in my name so that the Father maybe glorified in the Son. 14- If in my name you ask me for anything, I will do it."

John 14:15- If you love me, you will keep my commandments. 16-And I will ask the Father, and He will give you another Advocate to be with you forever. 23-Those who love me will keep my word and my Father will love them, and we will come to them and make our home with them. Whoever does not love me does not keep my words, and the word that you hear is not mine, but is from the Father who sent me."

John 15:7 "If you abide in me and my words abide in you, ask for whatever you ask and it will be done for you."

John 16-23a-24 "Very truly, I tell you if you ask anything of the Father in my name, He will give it to you. 24-Until now you have not asked anything in my name. Ask and you will receive, so that your joy maybe complete."

I believe that the search or pursuit of excellence is to know God and learn to use His power for a variety of wonderful blessings which are magnificent beyond words. I believe that to be better than good is to apply the laws of LOVE that bring forth joy, peace, good health and prosperity!

I truly believe the Holy Spirit, not only because I felt His Power many times in my life, but actually communicated with me. When I went to Harvard for a 3-weeks continuing medical education in 1973, right after I boarded the plane, I kept asking myself why I have to go for CME when I just finished my training five years before and what are the things that I don't know now. "Oh! What do you know about life son? Life is changing all the time. You should know that there are many changes taking place every year, because of the constant research going on not only in medicine, but also in technology. But ask me questions every day and I will help you." I was Shock but humbled to know that God's Spirit is with me answering questions that I will ask Him. Hence forth, I asked questions every day, and I always got answer. If the answer didn't come in my mind, I opened the Bible at random which was handy in my hotel. Where my eyes were focused first on, the verses were the answers of my questions. The most helped done for me was, He did an incredible surgery for me. I had a patient with a melanoma behind the right knee which I took out with removal of the palpable lymph nodes on the right groin. After a year, he came for a yearly check up and on the second year, it was shocking to find that his abdomen felt like a one big mass quite hard but not tender or painful. I told him that it is beyond my expertise anymore and that I cannot help him. "Oh, please don't ever say that!" I told him "Yes, truly it is now beyond my expertise." He kept calling me at least three times a week. I decided to schedule him just for him stop begging me. On the 3rd week I did the surgery. When I was washing or scrubbing my hands, I prayed to God saying that I can not do the surgery. Please Lord just use my hands. After doing all the prep and cover with the sterile drapes, I made a long incision. What I felt was just a huge solid mass inside his abdomen.

I could not feel any liver, stomach or the intestines. In a moment, my right hand inside his belly, was kept steady, and the cancerous cells ware falling like- tiny gravels into my hand. I emptied my hand each time it was full until no longer cells falling. It appeared then that all the organs are all palpable again and the entire abdomen appeared free from cancer. I closed the incision and the patient was free from cancer until the patient died of stroke 10 years later. What an unforgettable experience!

I brought with me 3 books: The Laws of Success by Napoleon Hill, The Greatest Salesman in the World by Og Mandino and Success System that Never Fails by Mr. William Clement Stone. Because of the very interesting story on those books, I almost read the whole night and never felt any sleepless sensation. I am as alert in the morning and anxious to get to the lecture room at the MGH. I bought one more book to read "The Cosmos." I also read a pamphlet about Dr. Kerlian Photography, in which he had designed a camera that will take picture of the human aura. In that pamphlet I learned the energy emanating from the ends of my finger which I use for healing pain in my body. This is the same as "Pressure Therapy" or Touch Therapy".

One Sunday, I asked the Lord why the numerous planets do not bump against one another. He told me mentally to visit the Boston Museum of Science which is only a block away. So, I went there, and I was very impressed that all the Natural Laws are not only mentioned but they are also demonstrated. I also saw and heard a baby's heart sound while still in the mother's womb; even saw a chicken hatched from a matured egg. To make it short I love the Boston Museum of science and I brought my children to see the place more than once.

15

THE POWER
OF PRAYER

Almost every people on earth have prayed many times in their lives. Even non-Christians even those living in mountains like the Indians, or the aborigines living in Australia. They have their own way of praying whenever they need some help, they believe to be a very Powerful Source. Nevertheless as we Christians, seldom, our prayers may not be heard and granted with favor by God. I am sure there is some requirements or a pattern that we need to follow so that God will hear our prayer. Here are some methods that the Bible has told us.

1. Pray only to the True and Almighty God who created the heaven and the earth and the fullness thereof, the source of life, the source of wisdom and the source of all perfect blessings.

2. You must have faith. "Whatsoever you ask in prayer, you will receive, if you have faith. Matthew chapter 21: 22. You must believe that God is able to do what you ask Him to do. "Without faith it is impossible to please Him. For whoever

draw near to God must believe that He exists, and He rewards those who seek Him." Hebrew 11:6

3. You must be one with God said Jesus, "If you abide in me, and my words abide in you, ask whatever you will, and it shall be done for you." John 15:7 this has the same meaning as Psalm 34:15 "Thy eyes of the Lord are upon the righteous; And his ears are open unto their cry. Identification with God's righteous purposes is essential.

4. You must resign to His will, and this is confidence that we have in Him, that if we ask anything according to His will He hears us. "John 5:14 Jesus set the supreme example and gets a Gethsemane when He prayed. "O my Father, If it be possible, let this cup pass from me; nevertheless not as I will, but as thou wilt…. Thy will be done" Matthew 26:39-12 As it is God's will that ultimately will be done, it is but wise and reasonable to yield to his will before you pray.

5. You must be patient. Says David: "I waited patiently for the Lord; and he inclined unto me, and heard my cry;" Psalm 40:1; Again, wait on the Lord: be of good courage and he shall strengthen thine heart : wait I say, on the Lord "Psalm 27:14 if all your prayers were answered immediately under the urgency of your pleading, you would probably be sadly disillusioned. Human vision is so limited that is it Always wisest to wait for God to answer us and when his wisdom in me deem best.

6. You must cherish no sinful desire says the psalmist, 'if I regard any iniquity in my heart, the Lord will not hear me. "Psalm 66:18 this does not mean that a person does not has to be perfect before he can pray. Over and over again God invited sinners to call upon him. But it does mean that unless you are sorry for your sins and are willing to be free from every evil thought, word, and deed, your prayers will not be effective. Sin separates men from God. Like dirt in an electrical connection, it stops the flow of power. Nor does he answer prayers of purely selfish nature says James : "You ask and do not receive, because you ask wrongly, to spend it on your passions" James 4:3 A prayer for a new car or to win a one hundred thousand on a TV program will not have a very high priority in the courts of heaven

7. You must be thankful. "Have no anxiety about anything, but in everything in prayer and supplication with thanksgiving let your request be known to God" Philippians 4:6" "Thanksgiving" connotes a worshipful state of mind, which is as important as believing in God's power to help.

8. You must pray in the name of Jesus. "What ever you ask in my name, I will do it, that the Father may be glorified in the Son : if you ask anything in my name, I will do it. "John 14:13 This means much more, then barley saying "in Jesus name" "for Christ's sake" at the end of a prayer. It suggests a desire to glorify God by asking only those things that are pleasing to Him and will be helpful to his cause. To pray in the name of Christ is to pray as one is to pray who is at one with Christ, whose mind is the mind of Christ whose desires of Christ, and whose purpose is at one with that of Christ.

9. Your prayer must be with utmost sincerity with humility and gratitude!

16

MY BEST PRESCRIPTION BEYOND MEDICINE

Shortly after I settled in Spencer, West Virginia I took time to read my bible and attended church regularly including Bible class every Sunday. I wrote a sermon entitled, "My Best and Greatest Prescription. " I wish now that I had recorded my entire sermon then. I made an outline and explained ever paragraph. The outline is as follows:

New life has begun by accepting Jesus Christ as your Creator and Savior. Ask for the forgiveness of your sins and love God with all your heart, mind, and soul. Pray that other will do the same. Include you enemies in your prayers.

Learn the commandments of God and His teachings, as well as the government laws of your land. Apply them every moment of your life as the guiding principles in the conduct of your affairs with your fellow humans. God states in the book of St. John 14:15: "If you love me, you will keep my commandments."

Know that your thoughts and ideas are who you are 99 percent of the time with your acts, whether noble or otherwise, make up the remaining one percent. This is so because of every decision made starts first as an idea or thought followed by an action. Perhaps the greatest challenge every day is having right thoughts. If we do not control those that are not pleasant or righteous, we suffer consequences. If we do the right thing, we will be rewarded with many good things. I believe it is important not to dwell on thoughts that are not consistent with the Divine principles or in harmony with our government laws or we may execute those unrighteous acts. Unfortunately, no matter how close we are to God, we experience more difficulties. I also believe that the hardships that we suffer are a test of our patience and faith to God.

Remember what the bible says in the book of Proverbs; "as a man thinketh in his heart so is he." "Matthew 5:27-28 states that anyone who looks at a woman with lust has already committed adultery.

Don't take your body for granted; special care for your physical body ensures that your earthly temple- were your thoughts and soul are stored- is healthy. Visit your physician regularly, follow healthy habits, and maintain healthy nutrition and exercise habits so that you may live healthier and longer.

Wake up every morning with a fresh outlook on life, a grateful heart, and noble mind filled with beautiful thoughts and ideas. Plan your activities for the day. Anticipate what you are going to do. Imagine good results. Be prepared to accept challenges, opportunities, and blessings. Resolve to do all the good works you can do today. While tomorrow may never come, look forward to a brighter, more challenging and rewarding day. Affirm that you are the most blessed person alive; you were born a champion. Don't doubt yourself. Believe that you were born to succeed and to receive good things because the Lord is with you and if you are with Him, all things are possible. Remember what St. Luke 18:27: "KJV. "I can do all things through Christ who strengthens me." (Philippians 4:13)

Try to forget the worries, problems, loneliness, fears, and negative thoughts in the valley of oblivion. Erase them from your mind and substitute them with love, understanding, faith, and confidence. Work on patience and enthusiasm, which are the great dynamic virtues because they enrich our lives. Thank God for the ordeals and miseries you have encountered. They are springboards of humility. They are the bridges and magnetic forces that bring you closer to God. Realize that problems and worries are blessings rather then burdens; they should serve as inspirations rather then failures and desperations.

Remember that genuine happiness is something that one cannot buy, borrow, or transfer. It is created within and it is the expression of a dynamic faith. It acts as a generator to move one's life with vigor and vivacity. Joy makes the heart and mind sing in perfect harmony. It is the expression of one's attunement with God. It is the expression of satisfaction, peace, and good health in both the material and spiritual world. Read also on my topic "prescription for Happiness" elsewhere in this book.

Remember that true wealth is kept in one's grateful heart, filled with infinite love. Real riches are one's thoughtful mind, beautiful thoughts, and wisdom. These are expressed through cheerful smiles, tender words, and noble deeds.

Search for divine and human wisdom that help to unravel the mysteries of life so you can better understand and better serve God, others, and yourself.

17

WHAT SUCCESSFUL PEOPLE HAVE

1. Successful people have faith and confidence in themselves. They are diligent, industrious, and strive for excellence.
2. Successful people are intuitive, and creative. They know their weaknesses, but they persevere and maintain a positive attitude until the problem is solved. They know that success is not attained suddenly, but by a strong will and persistence effort.
3. Successful people are willing to face challenges and, if they fail, they keep trying again and again.
4. Successful people don't procrastinate. They make thorough evaluations before they make a final decision. They use there time wisely and effectively. They don't waste time on failure, but use it for learning and problem solving.
5. Successful people maintain good moral attitudes and integrity, which are foundations for righteousness and truth.
6. Successful people eat healthy food and exercise regularly to maintain optimum weight. They realize that diet and exercise

are necessary to maintain a healthy heart, mind, body, and soul, which may influence their decisions.

7. Successful people are friendly, helpful, kind and cooperative. They believe in teamwork and understand the acronym: "Together, Everyone achieves more."

8. Successful people are humble, never arrogant or boastful. They listen to constructive advice.

9. Successful people are full of energy and zest. They laugh and smile often, and have good sense of humor.

10. Successful people have excellent foresight. They focus on the realization of their goals. Like artists or architects, they mentally visualize the outcome of their goals, which strengthens their enthusiasm and passion.

11. Successful people are optimistic. They study and emulate what inspires them.

12. Successful people have an "I can "attitude. The word "failure" is not in their vocabulary.

13. Successful people become excited when their friends and family members succeed in their own goals.

14. Successful people are honest, trustworthy, and dependable. They know that these attributes build excellent relationships.

15. Successful people are usually less stressed because they are enthusiastic and enjoy what they do.

16. Successful people practice gratitude. They show their gratitude through gifts of appreciation.

17. Successful people know how, when, and were to get help. They aren't afraid to ask for help during their journey toward success.

18. Successful people prioritize their goals and schedules. They always balance their lives.

19. Successful people listen well to professionals, such as teachers and colleagues. They listen to people with problems so that they be able to extend help.

20. Successful people learn from other mistakes, as well as from their own. They may never repeat the same solution, but look for thorough and well – evaluated options.

21. Successful people have a clear, written mission and inspire their company for continued improvement.

22. Successful people make a commitment to the realization of their goals. They are doers and performers more then talkers, because they believe that actions speak louder than words.
23. Above all, Successful people honor the Almighty Lord as their leader because they believe that God is their Creator and the source of wisdom, wealth, and other perfect blessings.

18

THE GREATEST THOUGHTS AND PLANS FOR EVERY DAY

Today, I will start and design a new blueprint for my life, which will help me develop enthusiasm, courage, and strength so that I can have greater power and better opportunities to serve my country and my God. This is why I was created and what I was born to accomplish.

Today, I will sit down and carefully assess the cause of my failures and successes in the past. I will find my weakness so that they may serve as the source of my strength. May my errors be the source to learn better; may my indiscretions and disgraceful decisions give me the courage to be more humble, prudent and, forgiving. I will consider my failures as my inspirations rather then desperations.

Today, I will learn something new and complete good deeds, so that I may have something to share with my family and friends. I will budget my time properly and wisely, so that I can have enough time for every worthy activity and will be able to achieve the greatest efficiency in all my duties and responsibilities. I will live today as if it were my last, counting every hour as the most precious moments of my life, so that I may accomplish what is worthy, but I will always look to tomorrow for a more challenging, brighter and greater day.

Today I will radiate to others the many good things within me. I will be humble and treat all people from all walks of life as special and the most important people I will ever meet. I will be cheerful and pleasant to everyone. I will be patient and understanding to those who have stubbornly erred. And above all, I will be kind, helpful, and sympathetic to those who need help, hope, faith, and strength.

Today, I will sit and reminisce over my childhood memories. I will think of the days when my mother held me in her loving arms and sang to me melodious lullabies. I will think of the happy years when I played with my brothers and sisters. I will think of the days when my father, whether rain or shine, took me to church to sing songs of praises to the Lord and to hear the minister teach us about the Almighty God!

Today, I will sit down with my family, especially my growing children, and I will teach them how to over come adversity. I will teach them and reveal to them the arts and secrets of success by inculcating in them the miracles of love, enthusiasm, persistence, and patience. I will emphasize to them the dignity of labor, the crowning rewards of honesty, and the many good blessings of happiness that will enrich their lives by practicing compassion and performing kind acts to other.

Today, I will discipline my whole life to exercise moderation and prudence. I will never indulge myself in any physical pleasure that is harmful to my body. I will search and abide by the rules of good, physical health and mental hygiene to attain and maintain myself in the best physical and mental health conditions.

Today, I will call on my friends whom I have not spoken to for a long time. I will ask them how they have been during the time in which we have not seen each other. I will tell them about how much I have missed their wonderful company. I will update them on the achievements of my children, their families, and share the good things I have learned and ask them, likewise.

Today, I will set a special time to commune with God. I will attune myself into perfect harmony with the perfect Universal Power. I will pray fervently for the world's greatest needs: the forgiveness of sins of all men, and a lasting peace through cooperation, love, and understanding for all people and all nations. I will pray for the life of everyone; a life full of abundance and good health.

Today, I will give back this day to the Lord before I retire to sleep with this concluding prayer.

Almighty God:

I thank thee for all the opportunities and blessings you have given me. Forgive me for all the sins and shortcomings I may have and those of my family and friends.

Keep me in thy strong and loving hands, that I may be shielded from all evil and dangers. Give me strength, wisdom, and good health so that I may be able to work and help your people. Continue to guide and lead them in the path of righteousness and to fulfill thy will.

Above all, may I be worthy to serve thee. Be my guiding master every moment of my life and, as I fall asleep tonight, I give my whole life to thee!

19

HOW A STUDENT MAY EXCEL IN ACADEMICS

Today is the best day of my life. I have discovered the right path to excellence in all endeavors. I am no longer content with myself as an ordinary student, for that status does not lead me to the best school where I can best develop my talent. I realize that my pre-school education is one of the most significant and greatest foundations of a good education. I say this because my parents and my elders, aside from the books, are my best teachers. They taught me everything they know, and still, they continue to guide and support me.

During my pre-school years, I was molded and programmed to always think positive, to believe that every problem has a solution, that all goals can be reached, and that I can be successful in any profession of my choosing. I was also taught the basic principles, of success such as hard work, patience, perseverance, honesty, compassion, cooperation, thoughtfulness, and other good moral virtues and values.

I have read many motivational books such as Think and Grow Rich and the Laws of Success by Napoleon Hill; Success System that Never Fails by William Clement Stone; The Greatest Salesman by Og

Mandino and his other books; series of books by Anthony Robbins; and many other inspirational audiotapes produced by Nightingale-Conant. These books created in me a new perspective about life and success. It's as if my eyes were opened wider to see the many opportunities I had never seen or knew before. I encourage everyone to read these books. They seem to give the reader the power to achieve one's heart desire. Of course, the Bible is the greatest book of all, because it contains the greatest treasures of life. It is the best map of the road to true success.

As a teenager, I realized that we are created in the image of God, and we are endowed with immeasurable talents beyond our comprehension. God gave us the authority to govern, to be stewards of all living creatures on the earth. Yet, most people are content with using only 5-10 percent of their brains. They are unaware that they have the potential to improve their quality of life.

So, how can we improve the use of our brains to 90 percent or higher? It is said that to be a genius, one must have an IQ of 145 or higher. Some also say that genius is 99 percent perspiration. I am more inclined to believe that the latter s true. That patience and thoroughness is genius. Many Olympic athletes and musicians such as Mary Lou Retton, Michael Jordan, Michelle Kwan, Mozart, and even Mr. and Mrs. Snider were not born geniuses. They made frequent mistakes at the beginning, but they were motivated and practiced tirelessly and persistently for years until they became their very best.

Even the discovery of medicines takes years, sometimes even decades, because of the trial and error involved in developing prescription drugs that are safe.

During my high school years and in college, I had the opportunity to observe many students who excelled in academics. I asked them what made them so smart. They reply was almost consistent. They had the passion to be better than anyone else. They worked very, very hard until they became the best they could be.

There was someone I knew who was not getting high grades. Some of his friends became scholars. He thought he was as smart as they were. This motivated him and he promised himself he would prove it. He studied harder and sure enough, he eventually got better grades then the scholars.

So, to excel in academics and other activities, you must change your beliefs and develop strong faith. You must have a strong faith, strong enough to withstand obstacles. With the help of God everything and anything is possible. He has given us the freedom of choice and as long as we don't violate His laws, what ever you conceive can be achieved. This, of course, requires proper discipline, enormous patience, and hard work. Today, we can get almost any information we need so that we may learn more by using the internet through the computer.

To be the best student you can be, always go the extra mile; meaning, read other books related to your school subjects. In every topic, there are several questions not easily perceived, but which can always be unveiled and answered. You should:

1. Always be punctual in attending your classes and be a model student.
2. Always be enthusiastic, humble, helpful, and friendly because these are the keys to leadership.
3. Always be patient and understanding.
4. Always be resourceful and always search for ways to improve.
5. Always anticipate common failures, so you may work to correct or prevent them.
6. Always seek advice and counsel from experts in order to avoid costly mistakes.
7. Always encourage and praise the others and never criticize anyone, for they too have the potential to become better and great.
8. Always encourage cooperation and teamwork, because it allows for achieving more. (TEAM)Together everyone achieves more.

To sustain such enthusiasm and intense desire to excel, strength and good health are required. Therefore, take good care of your body. Eat food with the best nutrition for health, including fruits and vegetables, fiber and meats, low or unsaturated fats, and take vitamins and mineral supplements, if necessary.

Keep your body clean and prevent contamination from transmissible diseases. If you are past the age of forty-five and above consult your physician for advice on hormones replacement. Exercise regularly to maintain the tone of muscles to burn excess fat and calories, prevent osteoporosis, maintain an ideal weight, and improve your cardiovascular, pulmonary system and cerebral system.

You should avoid the risk factors for stroke, heart attack and cancer by not smoking, not over drinking alcoholic beverages, controlling diabetes and hypertension, avoiding junk foods, and drinking plenty of water. Make sure to get adequate sleep to rejuvenate emotional, mental, and physical vigor and vivacity. Always maintain a good attitude and habits and never allow your temper and anger to explode. Take all the vaccinations necessary for the prevention of preventable diseases. Lastly, visit you physician regularly for a through checkup and health education.

Nutrition for the mind and the spirit is very important. What are foods for the mind? First, we should differentiate the mind from the brain. It is true that the mind is the function of the brain, and therefore, it is nice to know what foods are good for the brain. Foods that are rich with multiple vitamins are essentially good for the brain. The vitamin B complex is very useful such as B1 or thiamin, B6 (pyridoxine), folic acid, and B12; also fish oil, Lipoic acid, vitamin E complex, vitamin C ester, and many super anti-oxidants. Fresh fruits are excellent foods for the brain such as blueberries, blackberries, cranberries, and oranges.

The mind and the spirit are closely related. We should feed the mind with many inspirational books. There are many books on the market today that deal with success, and solving problems and worries. There are medical books that deal with depression, anxiety, and many other physical and mental problems. They are written for lay people without using complicated medical or technical terms.

The contents in the Bible are perhaps the best nutrition for the Spirit. There are many hidden treasures, teachings, and inspirational topics that lead to a successful life, peace, and joy. Review the Ten Commandments in the book of Exodus in your Bible. Prayer or communication with God is very important. Searching His laws and teachings, having a strong faith, and abiding by His laws and teachings are the key to achieving the best that you can be. Review also the Be-Attitudes of the High Achiever and Great Leader.

20

THE MAKING OF
A GOOD DOCTOR

Becoming a doctor is very challenging. It is difficult, in part, for the length of years to study—four years of undergraduate, four years in medical school, and another four years in residency training. If extra training is needed for a particular field of specialty, like thoracic and cardiovascular surgery, two additional years is necessary. Overall, it took me sixteen years of post- graduate education before I went to private practice.

Medical education and training are a very expensive investment. It requires unwavering patience, incredible passion, and talent. After four years of undergraduate education, one is not sure whether he or she is accepted into medical school. This is so because there are three or four times more applicants then what the collage of medicine can accept. Many applicants do not meet the requirements because of insufficient grades, traits revealed during the interview, lack of focus in extracurricular activities during one's undergraduate years.

After four years of residency, other questions arise as to where you will practice. Should you join a group practice? If you decide to practice on your own, do you have the means to acquire the facilities and equipment to practice? How much is it worth? Can you afford to pay malpractice insurance? Will you be able to pay the office expenses since Medicare, Medicaid, and insurances have limited reimbursements? These are the costs one should estimate before going into private practice. The best option these days is to be employed by a hospital, which practically pays for one's overhead expenses.

Other factors contribute to how one may be successful to practice his/ her professions. During my residency, I observed my professors and attending staff. I noticed some were busy while others had very few patients. I made rounds with them and told them what I had done for our patients.

I concluded that successful practices were based on good relationships with patients. I believe the greatest virtue of successful practice is the way the doctor establishes his/her relationships with a patient. A good doctor takes his/ her time to examine the patient thoroughly. The patient's illness must be explained, how it may have been prevented, and the best-known cure. Of course, there is no guarantee for the complete healing and one should make it a point that if the patient's health doesn't improve or the medicine doesn't help, the doctor should be notified. The patient should return as soon as possible for another visit and further evaluation. The doctor should always be honest, friendly and gentle. One should impart the impression that you really care.

I have a friend who, each time he saw one of his patients, didn't only ask about the patient's condition but also the entire family. He took his time as if that patient was the only patient he had. All his patients loved him and told all of their friends what a wonderful doctor he was. The doctor is now retired. Over the years, I made an outline as to what virtues make "THE GREAT DOCTOR." Here is what I have discovered:

T   Trustworthy. A good provider must be trusted, dependable and faithful to their patients and profession.

H   Honest. A physician must be honest and sincere for these patients to gain confidence.

E   Enthusiastic. Doctors must show a warm interest in helping a patient, whatever problems he or she might have.

G   Generous and Gentle. Doctors should be gentle and kind to their patients and make them feel that they have their patient's best interests in mind. Their voice should be tender and not rude. Occasional humor is mostly welcome; after all, laughter is the best medicine.

R   Respectful. Always be respectful and courteous to your patients regardless of their race, sex, and social status.

E   Efficient and Well- Updated through Continuing Education. The doctor should have other resources and other experts to consult when attending to difficult cases.

A   Attentive. Always listen carefully to the problems of the patients. Poor attentions and in incomplete medical history may lead to misunderstanding, misdiagnosis, discontentment and disappointment of the patient, especially if the doctor didn't ask what other problems he/she has.

T   Thorough. Incomplete physical examinations and history are the causes of many misdiagnosis Thoroughness minimizes the danger of a wrong diagnosis and inappropriate medication.

D Dedicated. This requires patience and perseverance in the overall care of a physician's patients, as well as the profession as a whole. Critical patient care requires energy, talent, and devotion in order to heal. Also, motivating and educating patients help them to have better health.

O Outstanding. It is good to be extraordinary in ones chosen field. It is important to be involved in worthwhile community activates such as educating and giving lectures to the public, and volunteering services in activities such as health fairs.

C Compassionate, Conscientious, Careful, Cooperative, and Competent. These five attitudes can "make or break" the satisfaction one experiences with their primary care physician. These attitudes are the best way to prevent malpractice suits.

T Tracking System. This simply means a routine follow-up with patients. It is commendable gesture to call and check how the patient is doing a few days after an examination. Otherwise, it may be good to ask the patient to come back for a re-evaluation, if they are not better.

O Organization. It is important for doctors to put things in their proper order to eliminate wasted time in located supplies. Orderliness in a neat and clean office is the first impression the doctor knows how to execute their plans in a timely manner.

R Resourceful and Responsible. It is a great responsibility to be a health care provider. Doctors deal with sick people on a daily basis. A minor mistake could lead to a terrible outcome. It is a great consolation to a physician to see that their patients get well. It is imperative that a good doctor knows how to execute his plans in a timely manner.

Finally, an active practitioner must spend adequate time to review his/ her current cases. It was my habit to review my day's work before I went to sleep. Questions to ponder are: did I do my best? Are there other options? Is there something I didn't write in my post op_ orders? Doing this is especially important if the patient is very ill. In the book, "The Ministry of Healing," the author strongly emphasizes that a doctor must take the good Lord as his partner, because He is the greatest physician. I always did, even now with my daily activites.

2.1

PRESCRIPTION
FOR HAPPINESS

"I am come that they may have life and that they may have it more abundantly." (John 10:10)

"A merry heart maketh a cheerful countenance: but by sorrow of the heart the spirit is broken."

Happiness is a state of condition brought about by the harmonious blending of the mind, spirit, and emotion. It is just like a musical trio playing three different instruments in a harmonious and perfect synchrony producing a sweet and pleasant melody. It is not self-gratification or physical pleasure. It is not just laughter, a smile, ease or comfort. It is not just enjoying what you are doing, but it must be the right choice, which doesn't hurt anybody or violate any laws. Sometimes it is very hard to define because both wealth and poverty have failed to bring happiness. It doesn't cost a penny; yet, it is the most sought after and the greatest goal in life, as well as the greatest feeling and form of satisfaction.

True happiness is deeply rooted in the fertile soil of contentment and is consecrated by sincere effort and by wise understanding and unfaltering patience. It is often felt after many tears or much perspiration. It is molded and perfected by faith, self-discipline, compassion, and noble deeds. Happiness is a great treasure you cannot buy, transfer, or borrow, because it is created within your soul.

To gain happiness, one must have to understand one's self by throughly analyzing every aspect of one's life. One should be able to eliminate one's undesirable attitudes and bad habits, as well as those evil thoughts harboring in one's mind. One should never dwell on worries or past unfortunate circumstances, for these things have been done and cannot be undone. One can be happy anytime and anywhere, whenever one makes up his/ her mind to be happy.

When negative thoughts enter your mind, switch your thoughts to the many blessings you have had in the past. Think about how fortunate you are to have been born in this world. Think of the enormous wealth and beauty of our country, the many freedoms you enjoy, including freedom of speech, freedom of the press, freedom to assemble, freedom to choose your business, freedom to vote or run for public office, and most importantly, the freedom to vote or run for public office, and most importantly, freedom to worship God. Think about the numerous conveniences available to you that are not available in some developing countries such as televisions, washing machines, cell phones, computer, plumbing, electricity, cars, and public transportation that you can use whenever you wish. One can also enjoy beautiful parks, museums, movies, libraries, and many other conveniences. When you dwell on these things, you begin to feel very grateful to God for the many blessings He has provided you! Allow whatever mistakes, shortcomings, or unrighteous acts you have committed to serve as lessons for discipline and prudence, as well as inspiration for creative thinking and problem solving. Think of the many possibilities and opportunities awaiting you now and tomorrow.

Life has many cycles. It has ups and downs and has many roads along its journey. We must look far beyond what our eyes can see in order to be able to perceive and follow the right road. There are many temptations, signs, and confusing labels in this world, and if we are not careful, we may end up following the wrong direction and suffer great devastation and misery.

Nothing in the Universe is constant. The only constant thing is the change that takes place from moment to moment. Today maybe cloudy and chilly, but tomorrow the sun may shine brightly. The roses may bloom and the birds sing in ecstasy. So, take this moment to attune yourself to the beauties that surround you. Bow your head before heaven and express your eternal gratitude to God who provides you with a wonderful day and other opportunities for a better and happier life. Always think positively. Always look forward to a brighter future, and always think of the magnificent and wonderful beauty of the Universe and the enormous, unfailing love that God has for you. Plant the seeds of love and divine wisdom into your heart and mind and let them grow and flourish with kind words and caring hands. Before you know it, you will find yourself teeming with joy and happiness.

To gain happiness, one must be able to control not only his actions, but also his feeling and thoughts, and blend them into perfect harmony, which results in simplicity and contentment. To gain happiness, one must adhere to the laws of divine Providence, the Golden Rule, and good moral values, and stay away from temptation and destructive self-gratification. To gain happiness, one must be able to distinguish between right and wrong, correct the wrong, and be able to stand up once he has fallen. He must be able to smile during pain and crisis. Because of his faith and resourcefulness, he should be able to "convert his scars into stars" as Dr. Robert Schuler has said. He was the famous minister of the crystal Cathedral Church in Orange Grove, CA. One should understand and affirm that happiness comes after one has overcome many failures and miseries due to faith, confidence, patience, and dedication.

To gain happiness, one must be capable of forgetting one's lost loved ones. Because we are deeply and emotionally attached to those whom we loved and lost, such as a husband or wife; it is natural that we feel sad. We ought to remember that death is inevitable. Physical life has its beginning and its end. Being lonely is not going to chance the physical death. Sometimes, to a patient who suffers constant pain due to incurable illness, death is much preferable then living. Hence, one should comfort one's self because the loved one is no longer living in miserable pain.

To gain happiness, nourish the mind by reading inspirational and motivational books. Learning is a lifelong journey. It should be a commitment to adjust and adopt one's self to improving the environment. We should focus, study, learn, and do the things that make life better. This is what our loving God wants us to be and do.

To gain happiness, one must be able to exercise the freedom to pursue happiness. In past years, in China and Russia, there was no freedom of religion. One was not allowed to practice religion or worship freely. They could not gather together in a church to pray to God. Thank God, things have now changed. There are missionaries teaching to worship God in hidden temples or churches regardless of their religious sect.

More on happiness as quoted from the notes of Dr. Kind N. Loving Jr. "Happiness is the joy of sending flowers to a friend or a loved one with a card that states, 'Every leaf and petal of these flowers express how much I long to hear from you; how much I long to closely embrace you that you may feel the pulsating love emitting from every beat of my heart.'

"Happiness is something I cannot define. Although I lost my hearing in one ear, I still have the other one to appreciate the melodious songs of birds, the sound of the crickets, the sound of the gentle breeze as the soft wind passes by, and to hear the pulsating sound of the ocean waves.

"Happiness is that sense of gratitude that although I lost the vision of my one eye, I still have one left to appreciate the beauty of a rose, the multi-colored leaves of different trees during autumn, as well as the magnificent and spectacular national parks in USA, and to be able to see the millions stars hanging in the heavenly sky.

"Happiness is the sense of gratitude that although I am disabled and paralyzed, I still have a motorized wheelchair to allow me to move around and a loving wife to extend all her loving heart and soul to assist and provide many things that I need.

"Happiness is a sense of joy that, although I have aged, I still remember the many joys of having seen my grandchildren growing healthy, going to church, and learning about God, His teachings, and their fear to deviate from the right path. I still enjoy and understand the evolution of the growing beautiful world, the progress of technology that makes life better in many ways. I still feel and understand the steadfast love of the Almighty God and continue to gain new information, which I can use to inspire others.

"Happiness is a special gift seeing that my children received good educations and are practicing their professions to the best they can be and not forgetting their brother, sisters, and parents, yet inspiring others for the glory of our Creator and Savior.

"Happiness is a joy that evolves from the little things that someone shared, not because of their material value, but by the unmeasured loving thoughtfulness of faithful and caring friend.

"Happiness is most felt after having lived over a great devastating misery- be it an injury or sickness or the loss of the most loving spouse.

"Happiness is a joy of knowing and seeing the many charitable foundations helping many needy people and other poor countries; the abundance and wealth of this country and the good leaders blessed with wisdom to lead this democratic country.

"Happiness is a joy with tears knowing that the Holy Spirit, which you cannot see, but exists in your mind, stores enormous love in your heart emitting its energy to every fiber of your soul making your life so peaceful, undefined by any words.

"Finally, happiness is the greatest gift and blessing that one has regardless of gender, social status, race, and beliefs, because we have a most loving and forgiving God who is the Source of wisdom, good health, peace, and everlasting joy."

Indeed, true and lasting happiness is the result of a healthy, mental attitude, a grateful spirit, a clear conscience with contentment and satisfaction, and a heart full of love, all of which are perfect blessings from our gracious Almighty God!

In another way of concluding, HAPPINESS stands for.

H   Healthy body, mind and soul.

A   Active in various affairs not only in his/her domestic duties or hobbies and professions, but also to some charitable organizations.

P   Peaceful attitudes leading to a peaceful life.

P   Prudence and perseverance leading to righteousness.

Dr. Herminio L. Gamponia, MD

I   Industrious and inspired about living in fullness despite many handicaps.

N   Noble in thoughts and in actions leading to integrity.

E   Enthusiastic to do everything good.

S   Sincere in all her/ his motives and actions.

S   Slow to anger in what one does.

22

THE MEANING AND POWER OF FAITH

Faith is probably best defined in the book of Hebrews 11:1: "Now faith is the substance of things hoped for, the evidence of things not seen." How can faith move mountains or cure illnesses? How is it that faith can transform or make things happen, things that once seemed impossible to do? Was or is Jesus Christ the only person who did the impossible things? Wasn't Peter also able to cure a lot of illnesses during his apostolic time, as found in the Bible in Acts 3:7-9?

A lame man was brought to the gate of the temple to ask for alms every day and Peter said to him, "silver and gold have I none; but such as I have given thee; In the name of Jesus Christ of Nazareth rise up and walk. And he took him by the right hand, and lifted him up; and immediately his feet and ankle bones received strength. And he leaped up and stood, and walked, and entered with them into the temple, walking, leaping and praising God."

Perhaps, it was and still is done by our Almighty Creator who makes incredible and seemingly impossible events to happen. As the Bible says: "Jesus is the same yesterday, today and forever." He controls the directions of the winds and rains., and establishes all the natural laws of and in the Universe. He still heals and works through His Holy Spirit. How can one achieve or perform such things? If the Apostle Peter could do it, can we do it as well?

There must be an explanation. Matthew 17:20 says: "And Jesus said unto them, Because of your unbelief: for verily I say unto you, if ye have faith as a grain of mustard seed, ye shall say unto this mountain, remove hence to yonder place,' and It shall remove; and nothing shall be impossible unto you '"

Likewise, the book of Philippians states: I can do all things through Christ who strengthens me." Take a note on the following verses- Matthew 21:22 says: "And all things, whatsoever ye shall ask in prayer,

believing, ye shall receive." John 14:12-14 says: "verily, verily, I say unto you, He that believeth on me, the works that I do shall he do also; and greater works then these shall he do; because I go unto my Father. And whatsoever ye shall ask in my name, that I will do, that the Father may be glorified in the son. If ye shall ask anything in my name, I will do it."

In the book of James, the brother of Jesus Christ, states "Just as the body without the spirit is dead so also faith without works is dead." James 2:25,26.

Printed in the United States
By Bookmasters

Printed in the United States
By Bookmasters